MW01128751

EVERYTHING BOYS AGES 8-12 SHOULD KNOW

Understand Puberty, Build Healthy Habits, Manage Emotions, Handle Peer Pressure, Set Goals, Discover Passions, and More!

JAMIE MYERS

ISBN: 978-1-957590-40-0

For questions, email: Support@AwesomeReads.org

Please consider writing a review!

Just visit: AwesomeReads.org/review

Copyright 2024. All Rights Reserved.

No part of this book may be reproduced or transmitted in any form or by any means, electronic or mechanical, including photocopying, recording, or by any other form without written permission from the publisher.

FREE BONUS

SCAN TO GET OUR NEXT BOOK FOR FREE!

TABLE OF CONTENTS

INTRODUCTION

Every boy's childhood looks different, but there are some common struggles most boys experience. While your focus at this time might be to have as much fun with your friends as possible, there are some things to know that will help you stay healthy and active as you grow. In this book, you'll find answers to common questions about your body and how its changing, why certain everyday tasks are important, information about mental and emotional health, and some advice for personal growth.

Like every young boy, you're probably still trying to figure out life. You might already have a couple of friends that you go to for advice. Although it's good to have people to talk to, sometimes their answers might not be helpful; your friends are still figuring things out, just like you. If you're like most boys, you're probably worried about all the weird stuff that's going on inside your body. You may be too embarrassed to ask anyone about some of this stuff, but don't worry; that's completely normal! This book was designed to answer some of the questions you might feel weird about asking.

As you grow up, your body goes through all kinds of changes. To make it even better, your world will be changing at the same time! This can feel a little scary at first, and that's okay.

Think about each time you start a new grade at school. That first day is filled with excitement—and uncertainty. You have new classes, you might have new friends, and everyone—parents, teachers, and classmates—expect different things from you. Life, in general, can feel like that.

If no one talks to you about this time in your life, you might feel alone, but that's one of the reasons we wrote this book. Just like it's embarrassing to ask some questions, sometimes adults feel embarrassed talking about them!

This book can be helpful even if you don't read it cover-to-cover. If you have a question, take a look at the table of contents to find the section that might give you an answer. Some other good places to look for answers include your guardians, an older sibling or cousin, and the nurse at your school or doctor's office.

This book goes into detail, making it easy to understand how your body changes. When you're done reading, you'll know what to expect as you grow up and how to deal with and control your feelings. You will also learn how to develop a daily routine to maintain good hygiene and stay healthy. Personal hygiene, grooming, and taking care of your body are healthy practices to develop as you grow up.

In addition to these changes, this book will help you start to think about your goals and dreams. These will change over the years, but the habits you start building now can help you throughout your life. Hopefully, this book answers the majority of your questions and encourages you to learn more!

A NOTE TO PARENTS

As this book covers topics such as puberty and sexual development, we recommend that you read this book in full before gifting it to your child; this way, you know what conversations are likely to come from reading the text. The intention of this book is to help give your child a good idea of what will happen to their bodies and lives as they grow toward adolescence. With that being said, many of these topics require further conversations, especially those that have cultural and/or spiritual implications.

CHAPTER ONE:
WHY IS MY BODY
CHANGING?

To put it simply, your body is changing because it's growing; it's just doing what it was designed to do! These changes are the most natural, normally occurring things to happen to you, and everyone goes through this stage in life. They may not say anything about it to you) or even mention it at all), but everyone experiences these changes. In this chapter, we will cover some topics that may feel uncomfortable, especially since we're going to use clinical terms for body parts to avoid confusion.

So, what causes this change?

Both boys and girls have hormones in their bodies that cause them to grow. Hormones are chemicals in our bodies that send messages to cause something to start (or stop) happening. These hormones influence various parts of the body in different ways, depending on the age and gender of the person.

When you get to be anywhere between 9 and 15 years old, your brain will begin to produce these hormones, which will initiate changes, starting a process called *puberty*. In boys, these hormones make their way through the bloodstream and send a signal to the testes, telling them to begin the production of testosterone and sperm. The hormone *testosterone* is responsible for most of the changes boys go through during puberty.

The changes these hormones cause happen both outside your body and on the inside. Your mind is adjusting to all the new hormones at the same time your body is, so you might experience feelings of confusion or intense emotions you've never felt before when going through puberty. There's a good chance you're feeling anxious about how your body is changing, too.

Puberty typically occurs between the ages of 7 and 13 for girls and a bit later for boys, as we mentioned before. It's possible that some of your friends still look like kids while others have already started growing a mustache! This is because puberty happens at a different time for each person. Every person is unique. Your family history also plays a big part in when you go through puberty.

ADOLESCENCE

The phase when we change from kids into adults is known as *adolescence*. Adolescence usually starts around 11 or 12 and lasts until the early 20s — everyone is different, though, so don't worry if your experience is different. As your body grows into an adult body, your mind, perspectives, and personality will also change.

You have nothing to be embarrassed about; everything about you is fine. Keep in mind that your body is doing its job. Remember, your parents went through puberty when they were the same age as you are now. So, now that we know these changes in your body are normal, let's talk about the science behind puberty.

WHAT IS PUBERTY?

If you ask anyone your age what puberty is, you may get different answers and probably a *lot* of guesses. Simply put, puberty is when a child's body turns into an adult body. Puberty is the appearance of significant changes in your body. These changes will occur in three major areas: physical, emotional, and social. It's important to understand that it's not just your body that changes; your personal sentiments and relationships will evolve as well.

Some of the physical changes include hair growth on the face, underarms, or chest, a deeper voice, and the development of acne or pimples. Because of the influx of hormones, you might experience mood swings or intensified emotions. Your brain will continue to develop as well, which can change how you think about the world around you.

Everyone experiences these changes during puberty, but the changes will occur at different times for different people. For boys, puberty happens later than for girls; most boys see puberty changes around the ages of 10-11, and for some, it may only become noticeable once they are 13-14. If your friends start going through puberty before you, just remember that this is completely normal!

HOW PUBERTY AFFECTS YOUR BODY

There are several characteristic signs that you are going through puberty — some of them are easy to spot, but others aren't so obvious. From the outside, it can be hard to tell that puberty has started because the early changes during adolescence, especially in brain and hormone levels, aren't visible from the outside. You'll probably notice the changes to your appearance before you notice the other developments that come with puberty. Below are some of the things you might notice first:

Hair Growth: You begin to experience increased hair growth in your armpits. You'll probably start growing hair down around your genital area, too; this is called *pubic hair, and it*'s not always the same color as the hair on the top of your head. Some people grow hair on their backs, shoulders, or chests.

Increased Sweating: Everyone sweats, some more than others, depending on physical activity and other factors. In the genital and underarm areas, a new type of sweat gland emerges at puberty. Body odor can develop when the sweat this gland produces comes in contact with germs. Since you'll be sweating—and smelling—more, you'll need to shower more often as you pass through this natural period.

Maturing Teeth: As you grow and your adult teeth come in, the shape of your bite and the way your mouth looks may change. By puberty, most of your adult teeth have probably already come in. Kids typically get their second molars when they're 13 years old. Between the ages of 14 and 25, third molars (also called "wisdom teeth") might come in. These teeth could show up alone, in pairs, as a full set of four wisdom teeth, or not at all. This is often the time when different dental treatments start. Having a good tooth brushing (and flossing!) routine is extremely important after receiving your adult teeth.

Increased Height: When children—especially boys—are going through puberty, one of the most obvious physical experiences is a "growth spurt" (which is just a fancy way to say that you grow a lot in a short amount of time.) You'll get taller, and certain body parts, like your feet, will grow larger than before. Your body is expanding quickly as you're going through puberty; you might even think that your shoes and clothes are shrinking! This period of rapid growth lasts for two or three years. Sometimes, this process can hurt a little and leave stretch marks on the skin, depending on how fast you grow.

Increased Weight: It's completely normal to gain weight during puberty. This happens because some of your internal organs, like your stomach and intestines, get bigger. Eating foods with a lot of calcium and iron is a good idea during this time; these minerals help bones grow and keep your blood healthy, providing more energy, proteins, and vitamins that are needed to support development.

Voice Change: Your voice will become deeper, and as it does, it will fluctuate between really high and deep until you fully transition into your adult voice. Sometimes, your voice might sound a little funny and crack or break while you are talking; it can be embarrassing, but just remember that other boys are going through the same thing! This awkward phase will stop towards the end of puberty when your voice chords are fully developed.

Sexual Organs: The male organs and testicles will expand. During puberty, your penis and testicles will grow in size, and the color of your scrotum will gradually darken. *Erections* may occur, causing the penis to stiffen. This can be embarrassing while you're learning how to control it. Sperm production in the testicles also starts. When you get an erection, semen, composed of sperm and some additional body fluids, may be released; this is called *ejaculation*. Now that your testes are producing sperm, if you have sex without using protection and ejaculation occurs, you could get a female pregnant. You will probably experience "wet dreams" when you ejaculate in your sleep. It can help to talk to an older male that you trust about how to cope with these moments.

Sexuality: When you start growing up, your body goes through changes that can make you feel like being very close to someone in a special way. This is because of those hormones we mentioned earlier. When you start growing up, your body makes some chemicals that can make you want to do certain things that will make you feel good. One of those things might be having sex for the first time. Sometimes, people might start to like someone new and eventually feel love for them. They might also touch their private parts themselves, which is called masturbation. It's important to talk to your family about this, even if you feel awkward, as every family holds a different value system for how to approach sex and masturbation.

Oily face: Acne and pimples are an unfortunate side effect of puberty. Not all boys get them, but it's a very common condition. Your face, upper back, and/or chest may break out in pimples. Washing your face twice a day with mild soap and water can help a lot, and there are also doctors called dermatologists who focus just on the skin. The wonderful news is that most cases of acne improve, or even clear up completely, by the time a person reaches adulthood.

Brain Development: Brain growth is faster during adolescence than it was during childhood. During puberty, many neurons grow quickly, creating new pathways in your brain and allowing you to understand more complex ideas. The way these nerve bundles connect in your body changes, which makes it possible to think in more complicated ways—which is why school is getting harder, too.

There's a reason this book dedicates an entire section to puberty, and it's to help you understand that what you're going through is normal. It's something your body must experience, and you should not be ashamed of the changes. All your peers are dealing with the same transformation in private, so though it may feel lonely, you're not alone.

CHAPTER TWO:
PHYSICAL CHANGES

As we discussed in the previous chapter, changes in your physical appearance are completely normal as you move from boyhood to adolescence. The order and speed at which these changes occur are different for everyone. These were listed briefly in the prior chapter, but here we're going to give you more details on what will look different—and why.

GROWING STRONGER AND TALLER

Testosterone is a hormone that your body makes in your testes during puberty. This hormone is essential for boys to grow; it helps you build muscle and strong bones, grow facial and pubic hair, and develop a deeper voice. During boyhood, it is normal to grow about 6 centimeters per year. Right before puberty, this slows down, but then, during puberty, your growth will speed up again to the rate of about 8 centimeters each year.

How Tall Will You Grow?

How tall you end up growing depends on a lot of factors, but the biggest one is your family history and genes. Genes are like a blueprint that tells your body how to grow (you'll probably learn about them in science class or biology if you haven't already.) If you have tall parents and grandparents, you are more likely to grow tall, too. You can change the genes you're born with, but you can help your body grow by taking care of yourself.

During this time, eating a healthy diet, exercising regularly, and making sure you get enough sleep each night will help your body do what it needs to do to grow strong and tall. Here are some tips to help your body through this process:

Good sleep habits: Adolescents should get at least 9 hours of sleep each night. If you feel tired, make time to rest. Even if you don't feel like you did much during the day, your body is doing a lot of work behind the scenes. If you don't get enough sleep, your body won't be able to produce enough growth hormone. It doesn't mean you won't grow at all if you can't sleep at night, but it does mean it's important to try.

A healthy diet: There are many foods that can help support the development of your joints, bones, and muscles. Protein, probiotics, and micronutrients (vitamins and minerals your body needs) such as Vitamin D, calcium, phosphorus, and magnesium will help your bones, immune system (which keeps you from getting sick), and tissue (like your muscles and nerves) develop. Here are some really good foods to eat:

- Almonds
- Chicken
- Salmon
- Eggs
- Milk
- Yogurt
- Quinoa
- Beans
- Leafy Greens
- Sweet Potatoes
- Berries
- Fermented foods such as pickles, olives, and kimchi.

You should eat as many of these as you can, as often as you can.

Exercise: One of the really important things to keep in mind when growing taller is bone health. Your bones need to be strong to support your body as it gets bigger. One way to keep your bones healthy is through *strength training*. Strength training involves things like lifting weights, push-ups, and resistance training. These affect what's called *bone density*, which helps decrease the chances of breaking your bones or contracting other bone-related medical conditions like osteoporosis.

Growing Pains

By age 8, you've probably already experienced a growth spurt— and the pain that comes with it. The pain you experience will vary compared to your friends, and it will probably feel different each time you have a growth spurt. Sometimes, it might hurt more, and other times, you might not have pain at all. However, if your muscles are sore or your bones ache during this process, here are some ways to help soothe your growing body:

Massages are great for muscle pain. You can ask your parents for help or do it yourself. Using your fingertips, rub your legs (or wherever it hurts) with gentle circular motions.

Heat can relax muscles and tension in the body. Heating pads and warm baths with Epsom salts are both good ways to ease some of the discomfort. You can try taking a bath before bed or using a heating pad while watching television.

Stretching is a good practice, even if you're not in pain. When you stretch out your muscles, it keeps them from getting too tight and increases the blood flow throughout your body. If you stretch daily, it can help with pains felt during the night.

MOOD CHANGES

When testosterone increases in your body, you may experience mood swings. Sometimes, boys will struggle with anger and become more competitive. You might notice you're having more arguments with your family members or even your friends. Some boys will have a "shorter fuse" than others, meaning they can get angry really fast before even realizing that it's happening. Competition can also lead to issues if it leads you to engage in dangerous stunts to "outdo" your friends or pick fights. There are some things you can do to help deal with these intense emotions, though.

Is it Really Anger?

Sometimes, what you are feeling isn't really anger; it's other emotions being expressed as anger. Feelings can get confusing, especially when there are a lot of them *all at once*. One thing that can help is learning to identify when you're feeling any kind of extreme emotion and taking a moment to pause.

Step away from what you're doing, take a few breaths, and focus on your body. Oftentimes, you'll have lots of thoughts going on in your head at the same time, but these are separate from what you are *feeling*. Try your best to push your thoughts aside for right now; you can always return to them later.

Focus your attention on *where* you're feeling the emotion in your body. Is it in your neck, shoulders, stomach, or heart? Does it feel sharp, tight, warm, or empty?

Suppose you can try to identify *what* emotion it is after you figure out where you're feeling it. You might feel multiple emotions at once, like fear and loneliness. It can help to try and remember other times you felt the same way and what caused it.

Once you can tell *where* and *what* you are feeling, accept it. Just let it *be.* Try your best to keep your mind clear and take several slow, deep breaths. This will help soothe the emotion, calming you down.

This process will take lots of practice to get good at, and you'll no doubt make mistakes and maybe even lose your temper. That is perfectly normal, and it's totally okay.

Why Are You Angry?

We've talked a little about hormones and the part they play in your emotions. However, there are probably other reasons you're experiencing big emotions, too.

Not getting enough sleep is a big one. If you're tired, it's harder to keep your emotions in check. You're also going to have more decisions to make — and a busier schedule — as you get older. These changes can cause stress and frustration, which sometimes show up as anger.

Another big factor is feeling self-conscious. Feeling "self-conscious" is when you are hyper-aware of yourself and feel insecure, ashamed, or inferior. These are all fancy words, but essentially, it's being worried about how you appear to other people, whether it's your body or personality. Everyone experiences this, and it's important to remember that there are great things about you, just like everyone else.

How to Cope with Anger

At the beginning of this section, we talked about a way to identify your emotions and help yourself calm down before your anger gets explosive. However, there are other ways you can help yourself deal with emotions, too. As we mentioned, getting enough sleep is important to maintaining self-control; if your body's tired, you'll have less energy to think clearly when things get tense. Here are some other things you can do to help you cope:

- Listen to music.
- Dance away the frustration.
- Get yourself laughing with a funny video.
- Do an art project.
- Go for a walk or run.
- Take a bicycle ride, alone or with friends.
- Take slow, deep breaths for at least two minutes.
- Perform a series of stretches.
- Repeat nice things to yourself.

How Sports Can Help

Joining a team sport can help with both increased anger and strong competitive instincts. Physical activity expends excess energy in your body and produces hormones (like endorphins) that make you feel good. Exercise also helps keep your body strong and healthy.

In addition to these, team sports are a great way to build relationships with new friends, people who are going through the same things you are. Stress, loneliness, strong emotions, competitive tendencies, and health are all things that will improve with intense exercise.

If you can't join a team sport because of your schedule or your family's needs, you can always get a group of family members, neighbors, or friends together to play sports at home. Bicycling together, playing baseball or basketball, or even a good ol' game of tag or kick the can are all great ways to de-stress. If this feels too difficult to do on your own, start by asking your guardians or other kids at school for ideas.

CHANGES IN YOUR VOICE

Your *larynx* is an organ in your throat that determines how your voice sounds. Sometimes called the "voice box," the larynx is a hollow tube in your throat, just above your windpipe. Your *vocal cords*, two muscles that look like rubber bands, are stretched across your larynx.

When you breathe, your vocal cords open, relaxing against your larynx, which allows air into your lungs. When you speak, these muscles contract (or tighten.) When air moves against them, the cords vibrate, creating sound: your voice.

Something similar happens with musical instruments. You might understand what is happening inside your throat better if you take some time to pluck strings on a guitar and observe the way the strings vibrate to make a sound.

As you grow and change, these body parts develop, too, causing your voice to change. Eventually, you'll have a deeper voice, but while it's growing, you'll experience a lot of back-and-forth between high and deep pitches. It can take as long as three years for your adult voice to fully develop.

As mentioned in the previous chapter, this can cause squeaking, cracking, and breaks in your voice. This is sometimes embarrassing, depending on who is around when it happens. When it does happen, try to keep in mind that it's not a big deal; even if somebody laughs, most people are not going to notice or remember the incident, so try your best to just keep going. Here are some tips to help you minimize these awkward experiences:

- Drink lots and lots of water
- Try to speak at an even volume—no yelling!
- Use cough drops.
- Take deep breaths to help with your stress levels.

ACNE
AND PIMPLES

The hormones at work during puberty also make your skin produce more oil. Everybody has different skin types and will produce different levels of oil, but a lot of people develop acne during this time. One of the best ways to help with this is by creating a good skincare routine. Taking regular showers and washing your face twice a day (when you brush your teeth) is the best way to minimize the impact acne has on your skin. Here are some other tips:

Don't pick or pop. If you try to pick or pop your blemishes, you risk spreading the bacteria to other parts of your face and skin. This will cause the breakout to become worse and spread. It also causes scarring, which is much more permanent than acne. It might be embarrassing to walk around with pimples, but it's best to leave them alone. They'll go away eventually.

Use the right products. It will take some trial and error to figure out what works best for your skin. When it comes to skincare, asking for help will serve you well. Chances are that your mom (or another female relative) can give you some great advice. They most likely have a similar skin type, know the kind of products that work best, and can help you develop your own skincare routine.

Try not to touch your face. When you touch your face, you transfer oils and bacteria from your hands to your face. In addition to this, you're going to spread any bacteria on your face to other parts of your body. Training yourself not to touch your face will also help decrease your chances of getting sick.

If you need to pop a pimple or zit, you can decrease the negative effects by doing it properly. First off, make sure your hands are clean. Use cotton swabs instead of your fingertips, as these will absorb anything that comes out and keep germs from spreading. If the blemish is ready to pop, it will have a white spot (or "head") on it and should release without much pressure. Take the cotton swabs, and instead of pushing them together, use them to pull the skin away from the blemish. This will prevent damage to your skin, as it will only release the inside of the blemish if it's ready to pop. When you're done, make sure to wash your face really well to prevent the acne from spreading.

Talking to a doctor is a good idea for more severe cases of acne that might require stronger treatments. Your doctor will know how to help you or might refer you to a doctor who specializes in skin called a dermatologist. There are different treatment options, including oral medications (pills) and prescription creams.

Makeup isn't just for girls. This is something you'll want to talk to your family about before doing it. If you end up with a really embarrassing pimple, you can ask someone in your family for help covering it up. Some makeup products also have ingredients that can actually decrease the size of the pimple.

Use ice to reduce swelling. Taking an ice cube and rubbing it on the affected area can help reduce redness and the appearance of swelling around the acne.

Hyaluronic and salicylic acid are two helpful ingredients to look for in skincare products. You'll find salicylic acid in most products designed to treat acne, such as cleansers, toners, and creams. Hyaluronic acid usually comes in the form of a serum or lotion. These products probably won't get rid of your acne completely, but they can decrease the size and frequency of blemishes dramatically.

These are some of the physical changes you will experience and how to help cope with them. This time in your life can be frustrating, but it won't last forever. The more support you seek from people you trust, the easier it is to navigate these issues. Some places to find support include your family, your friends, your teachers, coaches, spiritual leaders, and online communities.

Do remember that advice from people your age might not be accurate, and more often than not, they're giving you their best guesses instead of facts. This doesn't mean they're intentionally trying to misguide you; it just means that finding older mentors is important.

CHAPTER THREE: THE REPRODUCTIVE SYSTEM

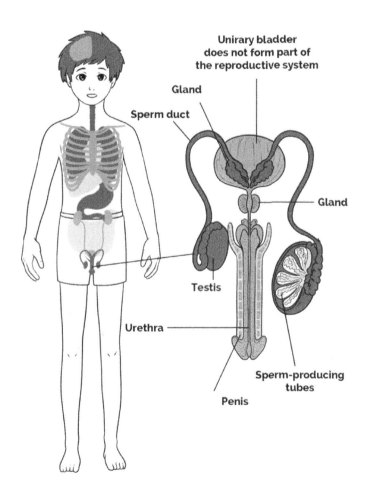

Unirary bladder does not form part of the reproductive system

Gland

Sperm duct

Gland

Testis

Urethra

Sperm-producing tubes

Penis

This is one of the chapters that you should talk to your parents or guardians about. Depending on your family's values and spiritual beliefs, they may have additional advice for you or might want to walk you through portions of this. It's important to respect their input. After all, they've experienced firsthand what you are about to learn!

What is Reproduction?

The process through which organisms create offspring that are similar to themselves is called *reproduction*. Our genes, unique carriers of human traits, accomplish this. In humans, these genes are passed down from the female egg and the male sperm during reproduction.

Unlike other bodily systems, the reproductive system is not necessary for the survival of an individual, even though it is vital for the survival of humanity as a whole. The male reproductive system is formed of both internal and external organs that work together.

What are Gametes?

The human reproductive process involves two distinct types of sex cells, which are referred to as *gametes*. The female reproductive system is where the male gamete, also known as *sperm*, and the female gamete, called the *egg* or *ovum*, meet.

Within your body, the sex organs are responsible for the following tasks:

- Urination (peeing)
- Producing sperm and semen

- Producing hormones

Remember how the previous chapters talked about the hormones needed to help you grow? Well, many of these hormones are produced in the reproductive system. These chemical substances either encourage or suppress the activity of organs and cells in your body.

THE MALE REPRODUCTIVE SYSTEM

Your reproductive system is made up of a complex network of organs, both inside and outside of your body.

Outside your body:

- The penis
- The testicles
- The scrotum

Inside your body:

- Seminal vesicles
- Prostate gland
- Cowper's (or bulbourethral) glands
- Vas deferens
- Ejaculatory ducts
- Urethra

The Organs Outside Your Body

The penis is the part of your body responsible for sexual activity and urination. It is composed of three main parts: the root, shaft, and *glans.*

The root: This is the portion of the penis attached to the wall of your abdomen, located just below your stomach area, around the waist.

The body or shaft: The body of the penis, known as the *shaft,* looks like a tube or cylinder. It is the main visible part, and inside there are three chambers. When you become sexually stimulated, blood begins to fill the sponge-like tissue inside these chambers. When these chambers are filled with blood, the shaft gets bigger and stiffens. When there is less blood in the area, the shaft shrinks and relaxes.

The glans or head: The *glans* is the point at the end of the penis formed like a cone, sometimes called the "head" of the penis. *Foreskin* is the name given to a layer of skin that hangs loosely over the glans. The opening of the *urethra* is at the end of the glans and is responsible for carrying urine and semen out of the body. This part of your body is very sensitive because it is filled with nerve endings.

The Organs Inside Your Body

Though the exterior parts of your reproductive system are pretty obvious—sometimes embarrassingly so—inside your body, there are many more parts you can't see. These are sometimes called "accessory organs," and they perform important functions. These organs consist of the following:

Ejaculatory ducts have two parts, called the *vas deferens* and *seminal vesicles*. The tube that pushes urine from the bladder to the outside of your body is called the urethra. The urethra receives the ejaculatory duct discharge.

The vas deferens is another tube that extends to just beyond the bladder. Its job is to move sperm to the urethra.

Seminal vesicles create a fluid that helps carry the sperm to the urethra. They are a collection of pouches at the base of the bladder. The seminal vesicles also produce fructose, which gives the sperm energy to move.

The prostate gland is a small organ in front of the rectum beneath the urine bladder. This gland functions similarly to the seminal vesicles as it helps feed the sperm and create the fluid that transports it.

Cowper's glands are tiny organs at the base of the prostate gland, on either side of the urethra. The fluid these glands produce helps lubricate the urethra as well as maintain a healthy PH balance. A healthy PH balance helps fight harmful bacteria or acidity from urine.

WHAT IS CIRCUMCISION?

All males are born with extra skin at the tip of the penis called *foreskin*. This skin is sometimes removed in a process called *circumcision, which* usually occurs shortly after birth. This is why your penis might look a little different than some of your peers.

Why Are Only Some People Circumcised?

Circumcision is extremely common in the United States; however, not all people get circumcised. The decision to remove or leave the foreskin is made by your parents at birth for many reasons. If you want to know why your guardians made the decision they did, it is best to ask them.

Many families decide based on their culture or religion. Some families have it done because it can be difficult to clean beneath the foreskin properly. Other times, the doctor recommends removing the foreskin for health reasons.

Is Circumcision Healthier?

Circumcision does not make a difference in health, but it can be easier to clean the head of the penis without the foreskin. The foreskin also protects the glans, which can decrease sensitivity for some people. If you are uncircumcised, it is important to gently pull back the foreskin when showering to clean the head of the penis thoroughly. Make sure to rinse off all the soap from beneath the skin. This will keep everything clean and healthy.

WHAT ARE ERECTIONS?

The term *erection* is used for when your penis gets hard and sticks out from your body. Although it is more embarrassing than helpful at your age, someday it will carry out an important function. Erections happen to boys of all ages. They can even happen before you are born, in your mother's belly.

When you hit puberty, you will experience erections more often. This usually happens when you are sexually stimulated, but it can also happen for no reason at all. It's common—and completely normal—to wake up and have an erection for no apparent reason.

As you grow up and your body changes, you might notice that you get fewer surprise erections and wet dreams. Other things, like how much sleep you get or how active you are, can also make a difference. Don't worry about how often you get an erection unless it hurts or feels weird. If you're worried, talk to your doctor or parental guardian.

How Long Can a Penis Stay Erect?

There's no set time for how long your penis should stay up. A typical erection lasts anywhere from about a minute to half an hour. Sometimes, your situation can make your erection go away faster or slower. *Priapism* occurs when a man's penis remains hard for more than four hours. If your penis stays up for more than four hours, you should see a doctor immediately.

Tips for Dealing with an Erection

Sometimes, erections will happen when you least want them to, and this can be embarrassing. Here are some ways to get it to go away:

- Light exercise like jogging or jumping jacks.
- Change positions: Stand up or sit down.
- Distract yourself with other thoughts.
- A cold shower
- A warm bath

HOW BABIES
ARE MADE

It is recommended to include your parents or guardians in this conversation as there are emotional, cultural, and moral considerations to this topic. The purpose of this section of the book is purely to answer questions about the *physical* part of the process. In its simplest form, a baby is made when male and female reproductive organs meet to pass sperm from the man to the egg in a woman.

What is Sperm?

Sperm are tiny cells from a man's body that are designed to join with a woman's egg to make a baby. When a boy grows up and becomes older, his body produces sperm daily. Because they are very small, they grow in the testicles in tiny tubes called *seminiferous tubules*. The little cells split and change until they look like tadpoles, with a head and a short tail. The head has things called *genes* inside it. In case you didn't catch it when we mentioned them earlier, genes are instructions that form the "blueprints" for how an organism is made.

The sperm go to a place called the *epididymis* to grow up and get ready to swim. Then they go to the *vas deferens* or sperm duct. When a man gets excited, his body makes seminal fluid. This fluid mixes with tiny sperm to make something called *semen*, which will come out of the head of the penis.

What is Sex?

Sex is when the male and female sexual organs come together. This results in pregnancy (the making of babies). Sex is a complex topic to discuss because it involves a lot more than just physical processes. There are emotional repercussions and health risks associated with it, too.

Every family also holds their own set of values about when sex is appropriate. For this reason, it is extremely important to talk to your guardians, trusted adults, and healthcare professionals about sex instead of relying solely on this book. This can be an awkward and embarrassing conversation, but it's one that every person has to have eventually.

The Meeting of Male and Female Sex Cells

When a sperm cell from a man meets an egg cell in a woman, they join together to grow into a baby. When sex occurs, and a man's penis enters a woman's vagina, the penis releases the man's semen (ejaculation) which goes inside a woman's body. The tiny sperm cells in the semen start to swim as fast as they can toward a tiny egg in order to fertilize it.

It only takes one tiny sperm to meet with the egg to make a baby, and *thousands* of sperm come out in the fluids from your penis. The tiny baby formed when a sperm fertilizes an egg is first called a *zygote* and has 46 *chromosomes*, which contain those genes we talked about. Twenty-three chromosomes are from the egg cell, and 23 are from the sperm cell, and these create a unique blend of characteristics from both parents in the new baby.

The baby starts to grow inside the woman's *womb*, which is in the stomach area. The cells in the zygote keep dividing, and it grows bigger and bigger until it becomes an *embryo*, then a *fetus*, and finally, a brand-new baby.

In nine months, the pregnant woman gives birth to a baby. Both parents are responsible for creating and caring for the baby throughout its life, which is why it is such a huge commitment that shouldn't be rushed. If you have questions, ask the adults in your life that you respect and trust.

CHAPTER FOUR: EMOTIONS AND FEELINGS

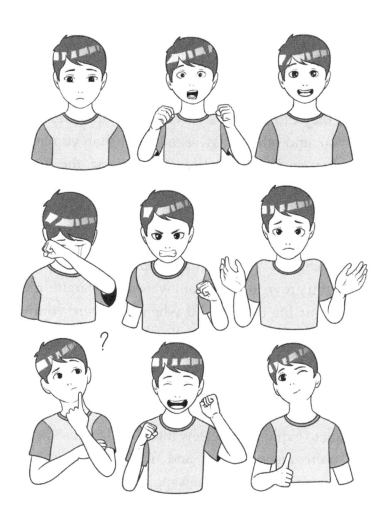

Emotional development is different for each boy, and it changes over time. Previously, we discussed anger and competition, but you will also experience a stronger sense of identity and/or show an increased desire to engage in sexual activity with peers.

Appearance

As you enter your teenage years, you may experience self-consciousness about your appearance due to the hormonal shifts brought on by puberty. You will probably develop an increased awareness of your appearance during puberty.

The opinions of others may start to weigh on your mind more heavily than they did previously. Some of your friends may seem older than you, and others may seem better than you at activities that you value, such as athletics or attracting the attention of others.

Family Interactions

You may notice that your relationship with your parents has changed. As you grow, you may not want your parents to know as much about your life as they did when you were younger. You could be told you've been unusually silent or distant from your family lately.

New things

You may want to explore some new interests. Increased confidence to take on more responsibility and make your own choices is common. You might pick up a newspaper or turn on the TV to be more aware of the world that surrounds you. You may become aware of an issue at your institution or community.

Teenagers frequently wonder about and experience all of these things. Don't be surprised that you may also seek some measure of freedom and develop an intense desire for friendships beyond the home. Some teenagers may exhibit negative emotions because they are frustrated by their inability to achieve their ambitions. Mood swings are also normal as your sleep schedule changes and your emotions continue to develop. It is important to remember that this is a phase.

WHY EMOTIONS CHANGE DURING PUBERTY

There are many factors at play in the changes you're feeling. Your hormones are fluctuating, for one. Hormones are those chemicals your body produces that regulate various functions, including growth, development, and emotional state. Your thinking shifts as your brain matures during puberty. Life changes might also bring about unexpected emotions.

One of the transitions you'll experience is moving from elementary to middle school. Although you will most likely know some of the students, the classes and schedules are different. There are new peer pressures for risks that could land you in trouble or have a permanent effect on your life.

Your family dynamic will also change as you change. Although there are a lot of happy and positive developments, experiencing so many new things at once is overwhelming. Remember that you are not alone. Every adult went through this, and most of the kids around you are experiencing the same things, too!

The Brain's Contribution

Brain development is a normal part of childhood and adolescence. A toddler's brain is about the size of an adult's brain, but it doesn't operate like an adult's brain yet because it's still developing. Brain development continues throughout childhood and doesn't stop until you're around the age of 25. Changes in mood can happen before you start showing physical signs, but you might not notice it at first.

As your body is changing, your brain is too. Neural connections, which help you learn new skills and ideas, will strengthen. Your ability to remember and understand things will change. Development will start at the back of your brain and work its way forward.

The front of your brain (called the *prefrontal cortex*) is the last part to develop. The prefrontal cortex is responsible for decision-making, problem-solving, the ability to think ahead, and controlling impulsive behaviors. This is part of the reason it is harder to handle bigger emotions. It is also why it's a good idea to get used to asking for advice from people you respect, whose brains are already fully developed.

HEALTHY WAYS TO DEAL WITH BIG FEELINGS

This book has already touched on hormones that trigger emotions; we've also covered how the brain's development affects impulsivity and decision-making when it comes to handling these emotions. Anger and aggression are the most common negative emotions you'll experience. They can cause fights, outbursts, and bad decisions.

However, you'll experience moments of euphoria and joy as well. A "mood swing" is when emotions go from one extreme to another rapidly; these sudden shifts can be overwhelming, especially when you first start experiencing them.

Handling Mood Swings

First off, remember that it's normal to feel overwhelmed and confused. It's a good idea to practice not speaking or reacting immediately based on your feelings. Getting in the habit of stepping away and calming down first will help a lot. Although all emotions are valid, and sometimes the reactions are warranted, your hormones are going to generate emotions that have nothing to do with other people at all. Remembering this can help you take a moment to yourself before re-addressing the issue.

Feeling Uncertain and Indecisive

Boys frequently feel doubtful about what they should be doing in the world and the position they should adopt. As you grow older, there is more pressure to act responsibly and behave in a certain way. Sometimes, figuring out what to do in these new situations can be overwhelming.

Accepting that change is a good thing will help shift your mindset. Things are different, but that doesn't mean they're *bad*. Feeling overwhelmed will pass. Anger will pass. Confusion will pass. It's easier to cope if you focus on the good things.

For example, increased responsibility usually means increased freedom. Your parents probably allow you to wander further from the house without them around. Your friends can do things that you weren't allowed to do when you were younger. Even your classes at school will get harder, but you'll get to learn new subjects and participate in group events like dances and extracurricular activities.

Seek out help whenever possible. It's common to feel shame, hesitancy, or nervousness when asking for help, and overcoming this takes courage and practice. Getting in the habit of asking for help often will make it easier. All around you are people who have experience and knowledge that can help you sort out life's problems. Parents, teachers, spiritual leaders, coaches, and older relatives are all great resources to help you figure things out when you feel stuck.

Handle responsibilities first. If you're ever in a situation where you have to choose between doing boring tasks, like homework and chores, and doing something fun, make it a habit to complete your responsibilities first. Many situations will arise where you will need to make a decision between these two parts of life. If you make it a rule to finish the hard, boring tasks first, you'll avoid a lot of stress and conflict in the long run. You'll probably even end up having fun later because you won't be worrying about your responsibilities—they're already taken care of!

Allow yourself time to adjust. These changes will take a while to get used to. It's important to be kind to yourself and just do your best. No one expects you to be an adult overnight, and you shouldn't either. This stage of life is all about growing and learning.

Exploring Your Identity

During this period in your life, you will most likely make changes in how you dress, talk, wear your hair, and think about yourself. It's perfectly normal to change your style frequently as you figure out what you like and don't like. Your parents might have some rules for you based on your beliefs, and these should be respected; however, it's normal to want to test them during this phase. It's possible that you feel like you don't quite fit in anywhere, but that's part of the journey during this time. Figuring out who you are and deciding who you want to be will take time. Below are some things you can try that might help.

Seek out role models. These should be people older than you that you truly respect. Finding successful people who carry the morals and values you admire will give you a frame of reference as you develop your personality. This could be anyone, including family members, historical figures, teachers, or religious leaders.

Try new things. Allow yourself the freedom to explore. Listen to new music, read different books, and try multiple styles of clothes. Pay attention to what things actually make you happy. Instead of focusing on what other people think, try to find the things that light you up with joy! These are things that genuinely align with who you are on the inside.

Consider your beliefs. While developing your personality, you should spend time thinking about what you believe is good in the world. Here are some questions to ponder:

- How do you think people should act to make the world a better place?

- What values do your parents hold that you admire and respect?

- What would you like to do differently and why?

- What are your favorite traits about your friends?

- What do you think makes a good friend?

- What are some things you think people should never do?

Questions like these can help give you clarity on the kind of person you want to become. Remember, you can change anything about your personality you don't like with enough research, guidance, practice, and determination.

Emotional Sensitivity

During this time, you may feel more sensitive than before. It's pretty normal to feel more aware of—and hurt by—rejection, judgment, and criticism. Although these things can hurt at *any* age, right now, you might feel like you are experiencing that hurt more often.

Some of this has more to do with being self-conscious than it does with reality, though. It can be difficult to figure out how much of it is your perception and how much of it is real. Sometimes, you might not even know *why* you are feeling sad or angry. That's okay! Here are some ways to cope and figure it out:

Journaling is a great way to let everything out. When you are feeling any kind of strong emotion, writing it out on paper can help you release it, give you time to calm down, and aid in problem-solving. If you don't feel comfortable keeping a journal, you can always use loose paper and throw it away afterward.

Try not to take things personally. This one is hard to do, but it will help you avoid unnecessary stress in the long run. If someone makes a comment and it hurts, try to remember that most people are not trying to be mean. They might not even know it hurts your feelings. For example, your parent or guardian could make a comment about a new outfit choice. All it means is that their taste in clothes is different from yours. Focusing on all the examples of them loving you, instead of the fact that they don't like your outfit, can help you remember that their comment isn't a reflection of your value as a whole.

Speak up. Take time to calm yourself down before you have a full conversation. However, if you don't like something, you can simply say, "I don't like that." Keeping your response short and concise can express your feelings while decreasing the chances of the situation escalating into a full-on argument.

Do something that makes you happy. When something unpleasant happens, it's easy to overthink the situation. Thinking about something over and over again can create a mental loop that will lead to the feelings escalating. Doing something to distract yourself will help prevent this from happening. Tasks that require you to work with your hands and focus your mind are the best. For example, you might play video games, go for a bike ride, complete an art project, play an instrument, or cook something yummy. Even though it's not fun, finishing your chores or cleaning your room while listening to good music can help a lot, too.

Seeking Acceptance

As you grow and change, you might long for the acceptance of new social or friend groups even more than before. It is important to remember that not everyone is meant to be in your close circle of friends.

Sometimes, you will meet people that you like, but it doesn't work out. You might try to do things to win their approval or affection. This is normal but accepting that not everyone will like you can go a long way when it comes to maintaining a sense of inner peace.

Instead of trying to force relationships to work, try to find people who genuinely like you for who you are. These are the people that make you feel comfortable, make you laugh, and are easy to be around. Sometimes, these friendships and relationships happen with the last person you'd expect!

Being around the wrong people is harmful to your well-being, confidence, and happiness. You can tell who is good to be around by paying attention to how you feel when you're around them and the way you feel afterward. Feeling insecure, ashamed, guilty, or uncomfortable expressing yourself is usually a good indication that those are people who should be acquaintances rather than close friends.

Bonding

When you find people who seem to "get you," one of the easiest ways to forge a strong bond of friendship is by doing things together. Here are some ideas on ways to get to know each other better:

- Study together
- Play a team video game.
- Bike rides or walks

- Play a game at the local park.
- Have a movie marathon.
- Play a board game.

MANAGING STRESS AND ANXIETY

Stress and anxiety are emotions that everyone has to deal with in life. Sometimes, people use both words to explain the same emotion, and they do cause similar responses in your body. When you feel worried or scared, your body reacts by putting itself into fight, flight, freeze, or fawn modes. This means you either attack the perceived threat, try to escape from it, go blank, or go into "people-pleasing" mode. Your body can experience things such as headaches, shakiness, shortness of breath, nausea, or body pains.

One of the most unpleasant things about anxiety, though, is the mental pain it causes. When something is stressful, nerve-racking, or causes fear, it is easy to run through all of the bad scenarios that can occur because of the situation. Even if these things don't or can't happen, the *feelings* behind those thoughts are extremely real.

Our body goes through these responses as a way of protecting itself. Sometimes, these reactions are there to warn us of real danger. Sometimes, the dangers are imaginary. Regardless of the root cause of the stress, if you experience a heightened sense of anxiety for a long period of time, it will wear down your body.

If you feel stressed or anxious most or all of the time for two weeks in a row, you should talk to your parental guardians and your doctor, as it could indicate a bigger health condition.

For day-to-day stress, here are some ways to cope:

Remember that it's temporary. One of the few things you can be certain of is that your circumstances will change at some point. If you are having a bad day, experience an embarrassing moment, or feel overwhelmed, it will eventually pass. Just like life is full of happiness, it is also full of unpleasant or uncomfortable moments. They will go away. You just need to get through it.

Focus on the present moment. If you keep getting distracted with worries about what's going to happen later or what happened earlier, try to ground yourself; focus on what's going on around you. If you're at home, remind yourself that you are *safe*. One way to do this quickly is to pay attention to your senses. Take a few deep breaths and list off the things that you can feel, hear, smell, taste, or see. Your brain can only process so much at once, and you can use this to your advantage.

Self-care is important. Although you should do little things for yourself daily, when you aren't feeling good, it is a great time to increase your self-care. This can be anything that helps you relax. Here are some ideas:

- Take a hot bath.
- Spend more time grooming your appearance.
- Create plans for improving your future.
- Daydream about better days
- Watch or listen to something that makes you laugh.

- Complete an art project.
- Finish a project you haven't had time for.
- Watch a movie.
- Enjoy a video game.
- Spend time with your family.
- Call a good friend.
- Exercise
- Read a book.
- Listen to your favorite music.

Take care of your body. This is also considered self-care. If you are feeling stressed or anxious, it is extremely important to look at how you are taking care of your body. Get extra sleep, drink lots of water, eat nutritious food, and make sure you are exercising. Taking care of your hygiene will also help you feel good and healthy. If your life feels overwhelming, returning to the basics is a good starting point.

Tend to your basic responsibilities. Once you've taken care of the basics — food, water, breathing, and exercise — you can extend self-care to other things too. Taking time to focus on your homework and get your chores done can help you rebalance. If you are religious, attending services or reconnecting with your beliefs can provide support and comfort. Spending extra time with your family and pets can feel good for everyone involved.

Think about the good things. When things go bad, it can be easy to forget the positive things. When you feel like this, it can be helpful to list out everything you are grateful for. Start with the most obvious, like having a roof over your head and food to eat, and then continue to think of as many things as you possibly can. Writing all of these out on paper is very therapeutic. You might even want to put the list somewhere you can see it every day, just to remind yourself that it's not all bad. If you struggle with thinking of things, ask your relatives or friends for help.

CHAPTER FIVE: GOOD HYGIENE

One of your responsibilities as a young man is a good hygiene routine. Responsibility for one's hygiene is a cornerstone habit that will never stop being important. When you're little, your parents help you with this, but as you get older, you'll have less and less involvement from adults. Your guardians will check that you've brushed your teeth and cleaned your face less often, but that doesn't mean you should skip doing these things. Skipping parts of a hygiene routine will lead to developing bad habits and long-term issues. For example, if you skip brushing your teeth, you'll have bad breath and get cavities. If you skip washing your face, you'll increase acne and blemishes.

What are germs?

Germs can be found in every environment. Germs, also known as *microbes or microorganisms*, can be found almost everywhere, including your own body: air, food, plants, animals, soil, and water.

There are germs on your skin, and there are germs inside your body. There are many harmless germs that can be found in and on human bodies, and some are even healthy! Other types of germs can make you sick. Germs can spread through a variety of channels, but these are the most common:

- Touching any surface
- Inhaling air a sick person has coughed or sneezed in
- Insect or animal bites

WHY KEEPING CLEAN IS IMPORTANT

Cleanliness keeps us from getting sick, increases our self-confidence, and can even improve our relationships. Poor hygiene can result in tooth decay, skin infections, greasy hair, acne, rashes, bad smells, and general illness. Social relationships are also affected by hygiene, and usually in not-so-obvious ways. Generally, people will try to be nice, but you'll still miss opportunities at work, school, and with friends if you don't take care of yourself.

Hygiene Becomes More Important as You Grow Up

Earlier in this book, you learned all about how your body produces more oil as you start to change. You will have a grown-up set of teeth as well. These changes mean taking extra care of yourself to prevent long-term problems.

Acne may seem like a tomorrow problem, but it's something that tends to get worse if you don't take care of your skin. Unfortunately, it is not enough to take care of a zit or pimple once it shows up. This is because the acne can start to develop *weeks* before it actually appears.

Nutrition, the cleanliness of your sheets and clothes, and your daily skincare routine will help determine what your skin looks like later in life. The more acne you get, the more bacteria around and on your skin; if it's not properly handled, it could spread to other parts of your body as well.

If you don't take care of your skin, you could also have permanent damage, such as scarring. This is one of the reasons why better hygiene is important as you get older. In this chapter, you'll learn routines and tips for keeping your body clean.

KEEPING CLEAN HANDS

Washing your hands is one of the easiest ways to keep yourself and everyone in your family from getting sick. Every surface you touch is covered in germs. Some of them are harmless, but others can cause all kinds of illnesses and infections. If you spend time in public places (like school), you probably touch all kinds of things.

One of the more common—and frustrating! —illnesses picked up as a result of not washing hands is conjunctivitis, commonly known as *pink eye*. If someone doesn't wash their hands then touches railings and door handles (for example), you can pick up these germs when you touch the rail or door after them. If you don't wash your hands, you could cause another person to get pink eye, which can rapidly spread through their family or to other people at school.

This is just one common example of viruses and bacteria spreading. Throughout the day, you might touch animals, playground equipment, railings, doorknobs, dirt, rocks, toys, and all sorts of stuff that carries all kinds of germs.

Use Soap and Water Every Chance You Get

Even if you don't use the bathroom, you should wash your hands if you have an opportunity. This will help lower your chances of spreading viruses and bacteria. To wash your hands:

Wet your hands using water as hot as you can handle. The hot water will help kill bacteria.

Add soap to the palms of your hands.

Scrub for at least 20 seconds. A good trick is to sing the "Happy Birthday" song while you scrub your hands. This is about the right length of time to make sure that the soap can do its job. As you scrub, make sure to get your wrists between your fingers, the backs of your hands, and under your fingernails.

Rinse your hands clean of the soap, and then finish by drying your hands on a clean towel.

Use a towel or your elbow to open any doors after your hands are clean. This will prevent your clean hands from getting dirty again and picking up germs.

Cleaning with Hand Sanitizers

In recent times, hand sanitizers have become way more popular. Where these are helpful if you can't use soap and water; they shouldn't be a replacement for washing your hands. If possible, using a small amount after you wash your hands is even better than just one or the other alone. It is a good idea to ask your parents to get you a small travel-sized bottle to keep in your backpack.

Nail Cleanliness

Additional hand hygiene involves taking the time to thoroughly clean and trim your fingernails, which may trap dirt and bacteria. Even if you take the time to wash beneath your fingernails every time you clean your hands, you should spend a little extra time on them regularly.

Keep it short: Keeping your fingernails short will help prevent excess dirt and bacteria from getting trapped. When clipping your nails, you want to cut them straight across and use a nail file to round out the corners. If the corners of your nails are sharp, they can cut into the skin surrounding them or catch on clothes and furniture.

Tools to use: The two main tools you'll use are nail clippers and a nail file. Ask your parents for a kit if you don't already have one in your house. Often, there is a small tool included in kits that makes it easy to clean the dirt from under your nails. There are also small bristle brushes available that make it easier to scrub beneath them.

Nail Infections

Infected fingernails or toenails can be painful and typically cause the surrounding skin to swell and the nail to thicken. These infections alternate between mild to life-threatening and often necessitate medical attention. Ingrown nails can happen if the nail is cut too short or at an angle. Although these problems aren't common, they can happen. For this reason, you should ask your parents to help you or look up a video online to make sure you do it properly.

CARING FOR YOUR TEETH

Cleaning your teeth prevents bad breath, but it also keeps you from losing your teeth or experiencing pain. Bad dental hygiene can lead to bleeding gums and cavities. If you don't take care of your teeth, they will rot, and you might even lose them. Beyond this, our dental health affects other parts of our body besides our mouth because of the many nerves located in the area.

You should brush your teeth two or three times a day. Most people make a practice of brushing their teeth when they wake up and right before they go to bed. It is a good idea to link this habit with something else to help you remember. For example, you can brush your teeth after every time you eat a meal. Or, if you go to the bathroom in the morning and before going to sleep, you can make a habit of brushing your teeth after you wash your hands.

To brush your teeth properly:

Put toothpaste on your toothbrush. If you can, try to find a toothpaste that has fluoride in it, as it helps protect your teeth further. Just remember that it is important *not* to swallow the toothpaste.

Set a timer for two minutes. This is how long it should take to properly brush your teeth. You can get a little timer from your dentist or ask your parents to get you one the next time they go to the store. Otherwise, counting works just fine.

Use circular motions. If you brush your teeth up and down, it can harm your gums. Circular motions will clean off the plaque. Make sure to brush both the front and back sides of each tooth, the tops of your molars, the back of your mouth, and underneath your tongue. You also want to brush your tongue and the roof of your mouth.

Use mouthwash afterward. Choose a mouthwash that has fluoride in it to help protect your teeth. You'll want to swish it around in your mouth for at least a minute or as directed on the packaging. You can ask your parent or guardian for help with this.

Flossing is Important

Our teeth are close together, and often, food will get trapped in between them. Although brushing is good, it's not enough to make sure your gums stay healthy and keep you from getting cavities in between your teeth. *Gingivitis* is the most common gum disease that people get when they don't floss. If you get this, your gums will turn dark red and bleed. They may cause you pain, too.

Choose your tool:

> **Dental floss sticks** have a short amount of floss between two points and a handle to make using them easier.

> **Dental floss reels** have a bunch of dental floss in a small box. To use this, you'll need to pull some out and wind the ends on your pointer and index finger on either hand. Be careful not to do this too tight, or it can hurt your hands.

Move the thread between each of your teeth. It is important to take the time to scrape the sides of each tooth and move the thread up into the gum. This shouldn't hurt unless your tooth is infected. If you are nervous about flossing, ask your dentist or a family member to show you how to do it properly. Flossing after you use mouthwash will help get the mouthwash between your teeth.

Issues Caused by Poor Dental Hygiene

Plaque: Plaque is a significant contributor to tooth decay and periodontal disease. Dental plaque, a layer of sticky film caused by leftover food particles, must be removed to maintain healthy teeth. It's not easy to spot dental plaque because it can look like a part of your teeth until there's a lot built up. Your parent can get you disclosing tablets or toothpaste at any pharmacy, which will stain the plaque on your teeth so you can see it, even if it's hidden. These come in a bunch of different colors, which can even make brushing your teeth fun!

Tartar: When plaque is left to build, it can harden and irritate the gums below the gum line. The hardened plaque is called tartar, and once it has formed, only a dental professional can get rid of it.

Gum Recession: This happens when the gums pull away from the teeth, exposing their roots. It can be caused by the buildup of plaque and tartar, brushing too hard or aggressively, tobacco use, or injury to your gum tissue, among other things.

Gingivitis: Redness of the gums, swelling, and even bleeding are all symptoms of gingivitis, which manifests itself in several ways. Luckily, daily brushing and flossing can often reverse gingivitis since it's the mildest form of gum disease.

Gum diseases: Gingivitis can worsen and progress to periodontal (gum) disease if the tartar is not removed. Having your teeth cleaned by a dentist or dental hygienist is the only way to get rid of tartar. Gum disease is made obvious by red and swollen gums that bleed easily, loose teeth, difficulty biting, and, in severe cases, tooth loss.

SHOWERS AND BATHS

The most basic argument for washing up daily is your body's sweat, oil, and odor. As you get older, your armpits, feet, and genital area will start to produce a stronger odor. Your skin will produce more oil, and your hair will become greasy faster. Dandruff can also occur on places like your scalp.

While all of this is completely normal, it's important to take a shower or bath at least once a day and to wash your hair at least once a week, depending on your hair type and texture. People with finer hair will need to wash their hair more often than those with thicker hair to prevent it from appearing greasy or causing acne.

When and How to Shower

You have probably taken many baths and showers throughout your life. As you get older, your parents or guardians will check up on how well you clean yourself less and less. Chances are, no one will notice how well you cleaned yourself unless you start to smell, but that doesn't mean you should skip any steps. Part of growing up is becoming responsible for caring for ourselves and our bodies, even when no one is watching. The habits you start practicing today will follow you through your lifetime.

Showers and bathing are not just for your physical health, though. They can also be a relaxing way to start or end your day. The warm water can help soothe stress and relax your muscles. Below are some tips for showering and bathing:

Adjust your water temperature to the perfect setting. One thing to avoid when cleaning your body is boiling hot water. While a hot shower can feel wonderful, using it too often can actually cause damage and make your skin drier. Showering in lukewarm or slightly warm water is recommended by doctors as a healthier way to stay clean.

Before using soap, rinse your body to get your skin wet and remove any visible debris. Sometimes, our bodies collect larger particles, especially if you play outside frequently. It's not uncommon to have sock fuzz between your toes or find grass or small twigs in your hair. Try your best to rinse off as much as you can and wet your body thoroughly. Even if you're taking a bath, you should rinse off your body before filling the tub to get off as much excess dirt as possible.

Wash your hair. You should talk to your parents or guardians about your hair type before choosing which products to use and deciding how often to wash your hair. Every hair type is unique and requires different care. If you can't ask a family member, there are online resources, or you can ask your barber for help the next time you get your hair cut. In general, you'll apply shampoo first. Scrub your scalp well, using circular motions to increase blood flow and help remove any dead skin, oil, or dirt. Rinse, and follow with any conditioning products. You may choose to let the conditioner sit in your hair while you wash your body, so it has time to fully moisturize the strands.

Use your body wash. Depending on your situation, you may have different soaps and tools. Some people use bar soap, while other people use a liquid wash. Some people use a washcloth to clean themselves, while others prefer to use a loofah. Regardless of what you have available, apply soap to some sort of cloth or loofah and scrub your body.

Start with your face and work down your body. As you get older, you might add special face cleansers designed to prevent acne into your washing routine. Start your shower or bath by cleaning your face and then work your way down, making sure to scrub every part of your body. One way to do this is to wait to rinse off your body until the end so you can see the parts you've already scrubbed by where the soap is on you. If you decide to do this, you will want to rinse your face before cleaning the rest of your body to prevent soap from getting into your eyes. Make sure to get easily forgotten places, like behind your ears and between your toes.

Don't scrub too hard. Although you want to get all the dirt off of your body, you want to avoid over-scrubbing. Scrubbing too hard can cause skin irritation or excessive dryness. This can become uncomfortable or look unsightly.

Rinse thoroughly. When you rinse, you should rinse until all of the products are completely out of your hair and off your skin. Pay special attention to your hairline, as it is easy to miss soap on your forehead or at the nape of your neck. When you are rinsed completely clean, you shouldn't have any bubbles foaming up in the water at your feet.

Towel dry when you are done. When you dry with a towel, it is best to pat your skin and hair rather than rubbing. Rubbing can cause skin irritation and damage your hair strands. It's also a good time to take your towel and use it to gently push back your cuticles on your fingers. At this time, your cuticles are soft, which makes it a good time to care for them. Ideally, you should have small, light-colored half-moons showing on the bottom of your nails.

Apply lotion to your body. While your skin is still warm, your body will absorb the lotion better and replenish any moisture that was lost because of the soap. This will help prevent dry, cracking, or ashy skin.

Do you need to take two showers per day?

To keep your body clean, you may shower twice daily if you work out frequently and spend a lot of time outside. A second daily shower, either in the late afternoon or before bed, is recommended by some.

However, if you are an indoor person and do not engage in strenuous exercise that makes you sweat, taking a shower or bath twice daily is usually unnecessary. You don't have to take two daily showers to keep yourself clean. Showering too often can dry your skin out.

With that said, if you participate in sports such as wrestling or martial arts, which require you to come in contact with mats, you will want to shower within three hours of leaving the mats, regardless of whether or not you sweat much. This is because other people's sweat (and germs) is on the mats, and you can develop serious medical conditions if you don't clean yourself off immediately.

How long should a typical shower be?

Once you've gotten used to the process mentioned earlier, you may find you can shorten your shower time. Ten minutes is usually enough time to clean your body properly. With that said, some people really enjoy their time under the warm water, and you can slow down the process as a form of de-stressing and self-care.

CHAPTER SIX: NUTRITION AND EXERCISE

Eating right and keeping fit go hand in hand with health. It's not just about growing big and strong; it's also about your mental and emotional well-being. At a basic level, your body is developing, and it needs fuel. Exercise will help strengthen your body and boost your mood. Getting enough sleep, eating nutritious meals, and exercising regularly is vital to staying healthy and growing strong.

WHY HEALTHY FOODS ARE IMPORTANT

For health and development, your body requires energy. You get that energy from the food and drink you consume, and that energy is measured in units called calories. Depending on your schedule, your eating habits will vary. Ideally, you would consume a handful of healthy, nutrient-dense food every two hours. This is rarely possible, especially if you are attending public school and eating meals at a set time every day.

Of course, everyone is different, and your ideal eating schedule may vary. If you don't have access to healthy foods as often, it may be better to stick to mealtimes and refrain from snacking. Ask your parents to buy snacks like trail mix, yogurt, fruits and veggies, and granola bars.

At your age, you probably eat three meals per day with small snacks in between. Although it may be tempting to choose easy, processed foods, it is extremely important to supply your body with nutrients. Junk food rarely has enough of the protein, vitamins, and minerals you need to keep your body functioning properly.

How does unhealthy food affect you?

Emotionally: Malnutrition (a lack of nutrients) doesn't just affect the way you look! Failing to eat healthy can make you feel bad, too. Lack of focus, increased anxiety, headaches, and irritability are just a few of the symptoms caused by a poor diet. If you eat the wrong foods, you'll end up hungrier faster too, and when people get hungry, they have a harder time controlling their emotions. That's what makes you "hangry"! It will also affect the quality of your sleep, which makes all of the symptoms harder to handle.

Fewer nutrients and energy: Weight maintenance isn't about eating less food if you want to lose weight or more food if you want to gain it; it's about moderation and getting enough nutrients. If your body is lacking something it needs, you will experience stronger cravings than usual, which often leads to overeating.

They make you sick: Foods with high sugar content are bad for your teeth and can lead to obesity, while salty foods can lead to heart disease, so it's crucial to restrict your intake of both. They can also cause or worsen gastrointestinal issues like nausea.

FOODS THAT WILL HELP YOU GROW

A balanced diet is what your body needs to grow properly. Healthy food for adolescents growing up includes fresh foods from these food groups:

Grains are things like bread, rice, cornmeal, barley, and oats. Whole-grain foods are better than refined grains because they contain more natural fiber. Seeds and grains are usually encased in husks or a natural fibrous packaging that protects the plant. These are important for digestion, and they help you feel full. When grains are heavily processed (like in white bread or sugary cereal), this additional fiber is removed, making it less helpful to your body.

Dairy or Dairy Substitute: Low-fat dairy products are sometimes preferred by people who are looking to cut calories for weight loss; however, while you are growing, you'll want full-fat products. Calcium, protein, and healthy fats are all important nutrients found in dairy products. Calcium is necessary for bone health and growth, and dairy or dairy substitute products are a good way to get calcium. This is why milk is usually a common part of breakfast and is offered as a side during lunchtime. Other sources of calcium include cheese, almonds, seeds, cereal, fish, tofu, kale, bok choy, and soy products.

Protein helps build muscles and keeps you full. Protein is one of the most important nutrients for keeping your hunger levels in check. If you have trouble satisfying your hunger cravings, your best bet is to increase your protein intake by filling up on protein-rich foods; you have a lot of tasty options to choose from, including turkey, chicken, bean sprouts, almonds, tofu, fish, eggs, beans, lentils, chickpeas, yogurt, and cheese. Your body also needs higher amounts of specific vitamins and minerals, including iron and Omega-3 fatty acids, which these protein-rich foods provide. The Omega-3 fatty acids found in many types of fish aid in the growth and development of your brain. The development of muscle and the expansion of blood volume in your body are both fueled by iron. Vitamin B12, which helps with both brain development and red blood cell production, is also present in foods high in protein from animal sources, as is Zinc, which is vital to your immune system.

Fats — monounsaturated and polyunsaturated fats, to be exact — are important for your brain's development. They are also important for maintaining healthy skin and hair. There are "good" and "bad" fats. Most fats that are considered healthy are naturally occurring and provide more nutrients than other fats. These healthy fats are found in foods like avocados, olives, nuts, seeds and fatty fish like salmon or mackerel. Unhealthy fats — saturated and trans fats — can increase your risk of heart disease, diabetes, and cancer. Trans fats are found in foods with "hydrogenated" or "partially hydrogenated" oils, and you should avoid these completely. Some common examples of trans fats include margarine, lard, fried foods, and fried foods. Think of fast food choices like cheeseburgers and french fries. Saturated fats, on the other hand, come from things like whole milk, cheese, and the fattier parts of meat and are okay in moderation.

Fruits and vegetables are packed with vitamins, minerals, water, fiber, and antioxidants. These nutrients are all important for protecting your brain and immune system, as well as your growth. Ideally, you want to eat 3-6 servings of fruits and veggies per day. Try to eat a serving with every meal or snack. If you don't like some types of fruit or vegetables, that's okay; you have a whole world full of different kinds you can try! There are also a lot of ways to fix fruits and veggies (or "produce") to make delicious snacks and sides. Celery and apples go great with peanut butter, and lots of veggies are tasty with dip. It's a good idea to make a list of all the fruits and vegetables you know you like. By stocking up on the produce you know you'll eat, you're more likely to increase the servings of fruits and veggies you eat daily. When possible, try to eat fruits and vegetables of different colors, as they each provide your body with different vitamins and minerals.

Many foods that contain minerals and vitamins such as vitamin C, folic acid, and potassium also contain dietary fiber, which promotes a clean-working digestive system and reduces the risk of constipation and other gastrointestinal issues. It can lessen the chances of developing life-threatening diseases like heart disease, stroke, diabetes, and obesity.

HOW TO GET YOUR DAILY FRUITS AND VEGGIES

Make them part of your breakfast. The first meal of the day is where to begin. Include fruit in your daily breakfast meal plan. Eat half an apple and add some berries to your morning cereal or yogurt.

Add them to every other meal. Keep your vegetable intake consistent by including them in your meals. Replace the normal with some variety.

Snack them up. Eat snacks made of fruit or vegetables to give yourself a boost. Fruits and vegetables are excellent dietary carbohydrate sources. You can increase their stamina-giving effects by eating them alongside protein sources, including peanut butter, cheese, or yogurt.

Find new ones. Get curious! There are always new fruits and vegetables to try. The human body thrives on change, so make it a point to experiment with something new every week. A new favorite could be on the horizon. Start with seasonal produce; it's a great way to add diversity to your diet.

Make them ingredients. Prepare your dish with fruit and vegetables as ingredients. It's a fantastic method for eating your least favorite vegetables without noticing their flavor. Make some zucchini bread; you can have your vegetables and bread simultaneously! Add chopped vegetables to your recipe. Vegetables can be disguised by adding them to other foods you enjoy eating.

MORE TIPS FOR HEALTHY EATING

Always eat breakfast. Breakfast is crucial as you grow. You can prepare your breakfast the night before and put it in the refrigerator, so you don't miss it. And, if you have breakfast, you'll be less likely to give in to food from other sources. Your brain can't perform as well if you don't eat breakfast.

Drink water. Water is often taken for granted, but it's a huge part of staying healthy. The majority of our bodies are made up of water, and it's a key component to all kinds of invisible processes going on to keep us healthy. If you're thirsty, you are more likely to experience brain fog, irritability, and hunger. One common symptom of being thirsty (even when you don't feel like you are) is to crave food. Your body is signaling your brain to try to find water in the form of food, which is why being thirsty can lead to overeating. Dehydration can also cause headaches and fatigue. It's a good idea to sip water all day long. Drinking a full glass before meals will also help keep you healthy.

Enjoy your mealtime. Pay attention to what you're putting into your body while you eat and focus on enjoying your meal. Switch off the TV and put away your computer, tablet, and other electrical devices. Distractions during meals make it easy to lose track of how much food you've eaten.

Be involved in preparing the food. Helping cook the food you eat allows you to see what goes into your meal. It will also help you maintain good eating habits as you get older and need to cook for yourself more often. Pay attention to how many vegetables are in the dishes you eat. Is there any way to make the recipe healthier? Sometimes, adding another vegetable or opting for fresh ingredients rather than canned ones can make a huge impact on the quality of a meal. Although you have little control over meal planning at your age, participating in cooking and food prep gives you an opportunity to ask your parent or guardian questions and learn about the process.

Avoid skipping meals. It's tempting to skip meals to control your weight, but doing so can backfire. Most people end up overeating later after a starving period. In previous sections of this book, we also discussed how many things can go wrong with our bodies if we are malnourished, thirsty, or hungry. It's much better to add in more healthy foods than skip meals.

EXERCISE IS IMPORTANT

It is normal and common to feel self-conscious about your physical appearance but try not to worry about how you look; instead, focus on becoming as healthy as possible. Exercise is a good practice, as it helps both your health *and* physical appearance. Exercise is a foundational building block to creating a healthy lifestyle, so the fact that you can change your weight, gain muscle, or tone parts of your body through exercise is just an added bonus. This book has already covered most of the ways physical activity impacts your overall well-being, including mental health, bone density, endorphins, and general stamina.

Exercising for appearance might help with short-term motivation, but if this is your only goal, it's easy to get discouraged when there are no obvious signs of change. This is why it is better to start a routine for health and wellness first and let everything else just be a nice outcome. Instead of exercising to look a certain way, exercise to feel strong, relax yourself, help with stress, or to achieve something specific like improving your mile run time for school physical tests or being able to bike 5 miles comfortably.

Sedentary Lifestyle

"Sedentary" is a term used to describe an inactive lifestyle. This means avoiding exercise and spending the majority of your time sitting or lying down. Between school and homework, you can often feel bogged down, and it's tempting to skip working out when you're tired. This is a problem that many people have, and it doesn't get easier as you get older (sorry!) You'll always have responsibilities that leave you drained, which is why it can be better to exercise in the morning before you lose motivation or join in some kind of fun team activity.

There are many health risks associated with a sedentary lifestyle. Although many of the consequences are easy to ignore when you're young, the habits you build today are what keep you healthy throughout your life. It is easier to stay healthy from a young age than to try to get healthy later because you *have* to.

Getting Exercise

We've talked a lot in this book about why staying active is important. At this point, we recommend that you take out a piece of paper and write down all of your favorite ways to get exercise. This doesn't have to be a "workout," though. It can be playing games like kickball, tag, or baseball. It could mean riding bikes or, going on walks with friends, or even dancing alone in your room! By making a list of all the activities that increase your heart rate or make you sweat, you'll realize how many options you have to choose from. Try to switch up which exercise you do each day for now. You can always try more structured workouts once the habit is easy to keep up with daily!

CHAPTER SEVEN: SLEEP AND REST

Sleep and rest aid in the growth and development of your mind and body. Like breathing, sleeping is a basic human necessity and is just as important as eating and drinking. While you're sleeping, your body and brain are hard at work restoring and maintaining your health.

WHAT IS REST?

Resting is not just taking a nap. It can also mean stopping what you're doing so you can give room for your body to repair and work at low power until you are entirely restored. Even if you can't take a nap, closing your eyes for 5-15 minutes can help you feel better and more alert for the rest of the day. Resting can also include relaxing activities that take a low amount of mental and physical power. If you don't take the time to rest your mind and body, you'll increase the chances of feeling burned out. "Burnout" is when you feel worn out, even with enough sleep. It's usually caused by trying to push yourself to do too much mentally and physically for an extended period of time. You'll need more rest during stressful times of life, like during finals or when starting a new school year.

WHY SLEEP IS IMPORTANT

Early in life, when a person is still growing and developing, they have a greater need for sleep. Infants often require more than 16 hours of sleep daily; even preschoolers benefit from daily naps. The *quality* of your sleep also impacts your physical well-being.

What to Know About Sleep and Rest

Your body follows a particular clock, known as a "circadian rhythm." The circadian rhythm is the usual 24-hour cycle of a day. Your circadian rhythm regulates the timing of hormonal secretions from your body. The regulation of this rhythm is a joint effort between two mechanisms initiated by the released hormones.

The external: The first step is that your body is synchronized with external signals. Light, darkness, and other environmental cues all play a role in influencing how alert or sleepy you feel. Light, for instance, informs the brain that daytime has arrived. Light signals can be from an artificial source such as the TV, computer screen, a light bulb, or a bright alarm clock. Your body secretes the hormone *melatonin* at night, which tells your body it's time to wind down for the night, making you feel sleepy. The concentration of melatonin in your blood reaches a maximum when night falls. Scientists think reaching this point is crucial in getting your body ready for sleep. Late-night exposure to bright artificial light can throw off this process, making sleeping difficult. Many teens naturally prefer later bedtimes at night and later morning sleep than little children and adults. Teens' melatonin production and peaking occur later in the 24-hour cycle, which may be a contributing factor.

The internal: The second step is an increasing desire to go to sleep the longer you go without it. The need to sleep is strongest in the evening when most individuals are asleep. Adenosine, a chemical known as a "neurotransmitter," used to transmit information between cells, may play a role in this need to sleep. The composition of adenosine in your brain keeps increasing while you're awake. Adenosine is metabolized in the body during sleep (which basically means that your body recycles it.) When adenosine levels go up, a person's need for sleep increases. This is also known as the "sleep drive" or "sleep pressure." The sleep drive keeps the sleep-wake balance or the right volume of sleep and wakefulness over time. The longer someone stays awake, the more they want to sleep. When people don't get enough sleep, their sleep drive makes them sleep harder and longer the next time they sleep.

What Happens When You Don't Sleep

Sleep is critical for optimal academic and social performance, as well as immune system function. Getting enough sleep can be challenging if you have many extracurricular activities after school. Lack of sleep can make concentrating, learning, and interacting with others difficult. You may find it harder to understand the feelings and reactions of those around you, and you could get angry, irritable, anxious, and moody if you don't sleep enough. The end product will be injuries, low productivity, and physical and mental health issues.

Benefits of Enough Sleep

Encourages normal development and growth: In children and adolescents, deep sleep stimulates the release of the hormone responsible for healthy growth. Muscle growth and tissue regeneration are two other ways this hormone benefits people of all ages. Both puberty and fertility are affected by sleep.

Restores your body: Sleep restores your cardiovascular system's health and function. Adequate rest keeps your body in the right state to support the changes your body goes through during puberty. Your body's defenses against illness and infection may respond differently if you consistently don't sleep enough, meaning that insufficient sleep messes with your immune system, making it tougher to fight off even minor illnesses. Sleep also plays an integral role in reducing the likelihood of developing obesity, stroke, cardiovascular disease, or high blood pressure.

Modifies the insulin response in the body: The hormone insulin regulates how much sugar (glucose) is in the blood. An increased risk of developing diabetes has been linked to insufficient sleep.

Balances hunger hormones: Sleep and rest aid in maintaining a satisfactory level of the hormones ghrelin and leptin, which regulate your body's appetite. If you don't get enough sleep, your ghrelin will rise while your leptin falls. As a result, you'll feel hungrier than usual.

Improves brain function and mental health: The brain is rewiring itself through sleep to better store and retrieve information. Your mind prepares for the next day as you sleep. It has been repeatedly reported that getting enough sleep improves cognitive skills, including memory and problem-solving. As a bonus, getting enough shut eye can improve your focus, judgment, and originality. Lack of sleep can also distort the functioning of various brain regions that control your ability to think, solve problems, manage emotions and actions, and adapt to new situations. Not only does it affect your social interactions, but it can also cause serious mental health issues. Depression, suicidal thoughts, and reckless behavior have all been connected to insufficient sleep.

TIPS FOR GETTING A GOOD NIGHT'S REST

Keep a consistent bedtime. Even if your parents don't enforce a specific bedtime, keeping one for yourself will significantly increase how well you sleep. When your body is used to a sleep routine, it will naturally become tired around the set time, which helps you fall asleep. Many people who keep inconsistent schedules struggle with falling asleep and waking up frequently throughout the night. It's best to keep this routine even on the weekends.

Exercise helps with sleep. One of the benefits of exercising is that it will help you fall asleep faster; lack of exercise is known to be one of the causes of insomnia. With that said, you shouldn't work out right before bed, as the hormones released by physical activity energize the body.

Choose a bedtime activity. The best kind of activity is quiet, relaxing, and doesn't require your phone or screens. By completing the same wind-down activity each night at around the same time, you'll train your body to get ready for bed. Some good activities include taking a bath, reading, meditating, or solving puzzles like sudoku.

Limit caffeine consumption. Avoid drinking caffeine after noon, as it will continue to work through your system for another eight hours. If you're craving a hot beverage, you can opt for decaffeinated tea instead. Caffeine blocks adenosine, which is the chemical that makes you sleepy.

Turn electronics off an hour before bed. There is a lot of research connecting blue and LED lights to feeling awake. If you want to fall asleep faster and stay asleep, avoid using electronics before bed. If you use a tablet to read before bed, use the "blue shade" or "nighttime" modes to minimize the effect of the light.

Only use your bed for sleeping. If possible, avoid doing homework or completing other tasks while in bed. Your brain will associate the activity with the place you do it, making it more difficult to fall asleep. It is also helpful to keep your bed and the area around it clean and clutter-free.

Tips for Relaxing and Resting When Stressed

Put things away, and intentionally make this your "me time." When you want to relax or rest, put away your phone, tablet, computer, TV, and anything else that can be used to communicate. If you are having problems with racing thoughts, play relaxing music or white noise.

CHAPTER EIGHT: MENTAL HEALTH

In some of the previous chapters, we discussed things directly or indirectly linked to the importance of mental health. At this point in your life, you're not only growing physically; your mental strength is developing, too, so it's important to care for your mind as well as your body.

Being an adolescent is challenging in the modern world because of how much social media affects your thoughts. While there are many benefits to social media, it can be tempting to view your friends' content and fall into the trap of comparing yourself to them. This may be one of the many problems you may face during this time of rapid physical and emotional growth.

While you're going through these changes, you're probably trying to figure out who you are and how to handle your increased freedom. Sometimes, the stuff people do can be super confusing, making it challenging for people to know what's normal—and what's not.

Sometimes, your hormones will make you feel super anxious and down, and, of course, you might need to deal with mental health stuff differently than grown-ups or even your peers. Everyone is different, so it's super important to be aware—and take care—of your own mental health.

MENTAL HEALTH AND WHY IT'S IMPORTANT

What is mental health?

Your mental health involves how you think, feel, and act. It determines how well we cope and process emotions like stress, anger, and grief and how we navigate friendships, make decisions, and set goals.

Mental health is just like physical health in the sense that everyone is born different; you need to nurture it just like you care for your body. For example, practicing mindfulness and coping mechanisms is the brain's equivalent to stretching; these practices help strengthen your mind's ability to handle stress. Just like people are born with physical conditions such as diabetes or epilepsy, people are also born with mental conditions like depression or anxiety.

Just like with physical parts of your body, there are doctors who specialize in aspects of mental health. There are also plenty of books and resources with information about how to improve your mental health. Just as with any other skill, you need to practice these techniques to see results.

DEALING WITH FEELING SAD

Although many emotions impact your mental health, sadness is one of the most common ones that people have problems with.

Even though we're focusing on sadness, most of the information in this chapter can be applied to any emotion. There's a lot of information in Chapter Four on how to handle emotions, too, if you want to learn more.

Sadness is a normal emotion. However, if you are feeling hopelessness and despair most of the time, it could be an indication of an underlying issue. Although it is normal to experience these feelings some of the time, if you are feeling stressed or sad for two weeks or more, it's a good idea to visit a doctor.

Tips for coping with negative feelings:

Observe your feelings. When you feel sad, write down all your thoughts and emotions and everything you notice about them. How do you feel? Where in your body are you feeling these emotions? What does it feel like physically? What caused these feelings? By writing out everything you notice, you can process your emotions and slowly become aware of patterns.

Engage in self-care. Earlier in this book, we gave you a list of self-care ideas. It is a good idea to add other ideas to this list specific to your likes and dislikes. Choosing activities that distract you, calm you, or create joy are all good self-care ideas. Self-care can also mean spending extra time on hygiene, grooming, and organizing your life.

Start by having a "growth" mentality. People who have fixed minds don't think things can change. Some people always feel the same way. They imagine that the way they feel is just how they are. Avoid these kinds of thoughts!

Take a few slow breaths. Try your best to focus all of your attention on your breathing. Whenever your mind wanders, bring it back to your breath. It helps to count to four as you inhale and count to four again as you exhale.

Take action as soon as you feel bad. As soon as you recognize you are feeling sad, stressed, or angry, start working down the lists in this book to help calm yourself. The faster you do something to feel better, the less likely it is for your emotions to get out of control. This will take practice, so don't feel bad if you don't always recognize when your emotions change.

Say nice things to yourself. Whether it's inside your head or out loud, it helps to repeat kind things to yourself. Listing off what you are grateful for and what you appreciate about yourself can help soothe you.

Prioritize your tasks. Figure out which jobs need to be done first. Learn how to divide a big job into smaller pieces that are easier to handle. Try to find a system to reduce some of your tasks until you feel better.

Tell someone if you're feeling especially sad or anxious. Lean on your friends, on your circle, when you need help. Find a network of like-minded people who can help you deal with things in a healthy way.

Remember, nothing needs to be perfect. Instead of always wanting things to be perfect, learn to be happy with what you put your effort into. Find a sense of pride and accomplishment in how hard you try rather than the outcome.

Stop what you're doing for a while. If you are feeling overwhelmed or frustrated with something, do something else for a while. For example, if your homework is becoming stressful and you feel brain fog, or when your thoughts become fuzzy, try finishing some chores or going for a walk before returning to it.

Take care of your body. A lot of emotional discomfort is caused by basic needs not being met. Try eating a snack, drinking a glass of water, and taking a short nap to reset.

WHO TO TALK TO IF YOU NEED HELP

During this time in your life, it's natural to experience sadness, confusion, and anxiety. Reading about these emotions is just a way to learn more about them and find solutions. Finding reliable people who can talk to and advise you is also essential. Your parents are the best people to speak to first. Outside of parents and guardians, trustworthy individuals include medical professionals, nursing staff, educators, coaches, guidance counselors, and senior family members. They are eager to respond to your questions and address your problems. Keep in mind: If you keep talking, you'll notice that your understanding of your feelings improves over time. As mentioned above, if you experience intense emotions most of the time for two or more weeks, talk to a doctor about your symptoms. You can also read Chapter Four to learn more about coping with new and intense emotions.

CHAPTER NINE: GROOMING AND APPEARANCE

Earlier in this book, we discussed the importance of hygiene and covered some of the basic aspects of cleanliness. In this chapter, we will cover grooming and appearance. Up until this point in your life, you might not have thought much about your appearance; your parents may have even chosen your clothes and haircuts for you. As you get older, though, you'll start to take more responsibility for how you look.

GROOMING IS DIFFERENT THAN HYGIENE

Hygiene is a necessity for health. It is a process that helps us prevent medical conditions such as bacterial infections, skin rashes, and gingivitis. Maintaining a good hygiene routine is non-negotiable for preventing sickness in the long run. However, grooming is not something we *have* to do to stay healthy. It is something many people choose to take seriously for personal expression and social perception. Social perception is how other people view us and, in this case, what they think about us when they see how we've chosen to look.

Although it's not good to judge people based on how they look, many people judge without even thinking about it. This is especially true in professional settings; sometimes, people can miss important opportunities if they don't dress properly. Learning what kind of outfit to wear in each different situation takes time and practice. For example, if you have a special event with your family, you're likely to dress nicer than if you're just planning to play outside in the mud with your friends.

Outside of special occasions, how you groom yourself and put together, your appearance is an opportunity for self-expression. It's a way to show people who you are. Although your parents and school will most likely have some rules for what you wear and how you keep up your appearance, there's still a lot of room for you to explore who you are as a person through personal style.

You can express yourself through how you cut your hair, what colors you choose to wear, what messages or patterns are on your shirts, and how you accessorize. Some people dress purely for comfort and function, while other people dress to stand out and make a statement. Both ways are great. At this age, you'll start learning what you like and what you don't like. This form of experimentation and self-expression will change and continue to develop throughout your life.

GROOMING BASICS

At your age, you probably won't need to take care of things like shaving or scheduling hair appointments. However, you should start getting used to the idea and maybe even practice. Combing and styling your hair is one area of grooming that you can start at any age. This chapter will cover some of the basic elements of grooming.

SHAVING

Although you most likely won't need to shave for a couple of years yet, you can still practice shaving with a bladeless razor. Asking an older male for help with this can make the process a lot easier. By studying and talking to males in your family, you can also get a rough idea of how much hair you might grow.

As you get older, your body will produce more hair. At first, it will come in patchy on your face. Depending on your genetics, it might get thicker and fuller before the end of high school. Not everyone will need to shave daily, but it is a daily grooming habit for many people. Even at your age, you can start looking at pictures of how people trim and shape their facial hair for ideas about what you like and don't like.

To shave:

1. Wet your skin and hair.
2. Apply shaving gel or cream.
3. Shave in the same direction your hair is growing to prevent ingrown hairs.
4. Use short strokes with your razor and rinse the razor after every stroke.
5. Rinse your face.
6. Apply aftershave and lotion.

HAIRCUTS
AND CARE

How often you get a haircut will depend on how fast your hair grows. Right now, your parents might cut your hair for you or take you to a barbershop, but when you get older, you'll take on this responsibility; for now, your only concern is deciding how you want your hair to look.

It is important to remember that different types of hair will style differently. For example, some people have fine, straight hair, while other people have thick, curly hair. Figuring out what kind of hair texture you have will help you find hairstyles that will look good with your hair type. Your guardians or barber can help you with this part.

Your appearance is what people see: Your appearance is the only aspect of yourself that people can see and judge at first glance, and there's no way to avoid that. Your appearance conveys essential information about your values, duties, ambitions, beliefs, attitudes, interests, expertise, and skills. Others are more likely to notice and appreciate your positive qualities and form a favorable opinion of you if you present yourself in an attractive, genuine, and event-appropriate manner. You have complete power over how you present yourself in any given situation, so you alone can help yourself.

It affects how you think: You can't afford low self-esteem because of your appearance. When you look genuine, attractive, and well-dressed, your thought process differs, and this impacts your interactions with others.

It affects your mood: If it makes you think differently, it will affect your mood. Improving one's outward appearance is a quick and easy technique to calm fears of inadequacy or rejection. You will feel more at ease, confident, capable, cooperative, and productive if your outward appearance matches how you feel.

It affects your behavior: Your mood is shown by how you behave, and grooming is part of your behavior. One of the efficient and easiest things to do to raise your spirits and productivity is to focus on your outward appearance. Your confidence, ease, manners, competence, and natural ability to perform your best all increase when you appear well-groomed, original, and appropriate.

Some grooming techniques:

Regular bathing time: Taking a thorough shower regularly is the foundation of good hygiene. The dirt and germs that cling to our skin can be washed away with a daily shower or bath using clean water and soap.

Oral care: It's vital to practice good oral hygiene. Bad breath, dry mouth, tartar buildup, and even oral, digestive, and cardiovascular disorders result from neglecting one's oral hygiene. The mouth should be cleaned thoroughly at least twice daily with a toothbrush and toothpaste as directed by a dentist. Your daily itinerary should include scraping the tongue, moisturizing the lips, flossing, and gargling using mouthwash.

Get used to manicuring: It's crucial to regularly wash your hands with soap and water because germs and bacteria can live in the cracks between your fingers and under your nails for days. Maintaining neat nails requires regular trimming. Remove debris, dirt, and bacteria from under your nails by brushing them with a

92

nail brush or washcloth. Keep germs from entering your mouth and other body orifices by keeping your fingernails clean. Nail biting is another bad habit you should break.

Avoid stinky feet: Sweat and fungi, most often athlete's foot, are mainly to blame for stinky feet. These can be avoided by maintaining a routine of washing feet and shoes.

Unkempt hair: Lice and dandruff can remain in your hair for a long time if you don't routinely wash it with shampoo and conditioner. We make a positive first and lasting impression on others when our hair is well-combed and styled.

Keep your diet well-rounded: Having a well-balanced meal plan is one of the nicest things we can do to keep our bodies functioning at their best. Clear skin and shiny hair are a direct result of maintaining a healthy diet and adequate water intake. It shields you from illness, too.

Proper sex hygiene and sexual health: It would be best to inspect your privates periodically because this will help you catch any changes early. Keep your pubic hair at the length you like, wash from front to back, and wear briefs that feel good. When bathing, uncircumcised men must wash under the foreskin. Check Chapter Three for more details.

Clean clothing and footwear: Grooming is all about making a good impression. You'll come across more confidently if you dress well. Choose your clothing, footwear, and accessories carefully so you may relax and enjoy the process. As a bonus, doing so improves your prospects and self-esteem. If your shoes or clothes are too tight, you may experience discomfort. If you have allergies, avoid cologne and essential oils. Instead, take more frequent showers and wear fabrics that allow air to circulate.

Be consistent in your efforts to work out: There is more to grooming than just how you look. Exercise has multiple benefits, including helping you keep a decent body shape and posture, protecting your heart, and boosting your mood.

Form healthy routines: It's not enough to only look and smell good; you may improve your interactions with others and how you feel about yourself by adopting positive behaviors like smiling, being polite, and helping others.

WASHING YOUR FACE

Choose an appropriate facial cleanser: Start with selecting a suitable face wash. Most people will advise avoiding using the same bathing soap you use for your body on your face. Use a face wash for your skin type to eliminate the day's buildup. During puberty, you know your body produces more oil, often making your face greasy. People who have problems with grease tend to choose foaming cleansers that also exfoliate. If you have oilier skin, avoid cream, milk, and jelly cleansers.

Keep your hands clean: Ensure your hands are nice and clean before using a cleanser. We touch all sorts of things with our hands, so they're easily contaminated. Since you will need to use those hands to touch your face, you want to avoid transferring germs from hand to face. Wash your hands often, and especially before you wash your face.

Apply your cleanser or agents: The substances we use to clean our skin are called "agents." These agents stick to the dirt and oils on our skin, making them easier to wash away. Follow the directions on your cleanser when you wash your face; some cleansers require that you wet your face first, while others recommend that you apply it to dry skin.

Use wet fingers to apply: While applying the face cleanser, ensure your fingers are wet. Then, use wet fingers to gently rub the face wash into your whole face in circles. This will mix the cleanser and make removing dirt, oil, and dead skin easier. Don't scrub too hard, as this can irritate your skin.

Use lukewarm water: Wash off all the soap with warm water that's not too hot or cold so your skin stays healthy. Avoid using hot water on your face; it's not good for your skin. It can mess up the oils that protect your skin and keep it healthy. When we use hot water, our skin can get confused and feel too dry and too oily at the same time. This can be especially tricky for delicate skin.

Avoid harsh treatment of the facial skin: Be careful not to tug, pull, or scratch your skin too hard; it can make your skin irritated, wrinkly, and saggy. Your facial skin is not as tough and can't be exposed to the same treatment as other body parts.

Wash twice: Depending on your skin type, you may want to wash your face twice in a row. It's best to consult your doctor when deciding.

Use a soft towel: After the final rinse, use a soft towel to gently pat — not rub — your skin dry. This is a simple step that might seem insignificant, but it's very important. Now that you have nice, clean skin, avoid drying your face with your bath towel or using a dirty washcloth, which can put germs back on your skin.

Avoid using artificial softeners and fragrances: You don't want to start adding chemicals to your face. These could mix with the oils on your face to clog up the pores, which may prove to be an issue. If these chemicals stay too long on your face, they could begin to produce odors, and you don't want this mixing with puberty!

Make use of aftercare: After washing, your face may feel tight. You can apply serum, moisturizer, or other skincare products that will add vitamins and moisture to your face. This will help your skin remain fresh and healthy.

Note: A healthy diet and drinking lots of water will encourage clear, healthy skin.

BRUSHING YOUR HAIR

During puberty, when your sebaceous glands are generating more oil, your hair might have a tendency to get greasy. The sebaceous glands sited at the base of each hair strand are responsible for the hair's shine and water resistance.

Hair Washing

Oily hair can be managed by washing your hair daily or every other day.

- Let your parents get you shampoo from drugstores or grocery stores.

- If you have very greasy hair, you should try shampoo designed for oily hair.
- Create a lather as you rub your hair with shampoo and warm water.
- Avoid harsh scrubbing since this will not help remove oil and may cause hair damage or scalp irritation.
- Rinse your hair.
- After you've finished rinsing, you can apply conditioner.

Brushing After Washing

Now that your hair is clean, let's focus on any tangles or knots present.

- If your hair is highly tangled or knotted, leave your conditioner in for a few minutes before rinsing, and use your fingers to gently remove tangles while the conditioner is in your hair.
- Wait for your hair to dry before using a brush.
- Don't tug or pull at your hair while brushing it.
- Brush gently, working out any tangles with your fingertips first.
- Start from the ends of your hair, then move up a few inches and continue combing down to remove any remaining knots.
- Keep brushing until your hair is detangled to the scalp.

When you visit the barber for a haircut, pay special attention to the items they use to style your hair. These may be good products for you to buy for use at home.

BUILDING HEALTHY SELF-ESTEEM

It's extremely important to invest in yourself early. Looking good leads to feeling good, thinking about good things, and becoming the best version of yourself.

How low self-esteem starts.

Sometimes, boys feel a little less sure of themselves during puberty. They compare themselves to others too much, feeling worried about their physical appearance. You might be skinnier, less muscular, more grown-up, shorter, taller, or even heavier than other boys in your classes or age group; you should understand that it's okay.

In some cases, as a result of puberty, your skin is greasy, your body may begin to produce stronger smells, you grow more hair around your body, and all these other changes could become an issue if you are not practicing good personal hygiene, as we mentioned earlier.

When you grow up, your body, feelings, and hormones change significantly. This can make you feel different and affect how you feel about yourself. Some teenagers grow faster or slower than their friends and might feel shy about their bodies; feeling like you belong can make you feel really good about yourself. Growing up can be challenging, but loving yourself and maintaining confidence is essential.

Building Self-Esteem

Being happy and staying positive often translates into your physical appearance and makes you more attractive to people. Try to practice optimism; it might seem silly initially, but if you keep doing it, you'll find that it helps. Try to think of happy thoughts instead of sad ones.

Sometimes, when you're alone, you might start thinking not-so-happy thoughts about yourself. If you're sad and can't seem to cheer up, asking for help is okay. You can talk to your parents, teacher, school counselor, or doctor. They can help you feel better.

Remember to take care of yourself. It's important to keep things clean and look nice. Remember to bathe, brush your teeth well, shave if needed, brush your hair, wear fresh clothes, and tidy shoes, keep your nails neat, and get your hair cut often. These things can really help you feel good about yourself. Don't worry! Putting in the effort to look good is not being vain; it's a form of self-care.

CHAPTER TEN: PERSONAL RESPONSIBILITY

You may have noticed that all the topics discussed in this book are meant to help you understand the growth process and maintain good physical and mental health. Eating healthy, maintaining good hygiene and grooming habits, getting regular exercise, and everything else we've talked about are things that you have to do. When you are in charge of doing something (or making sure it gets done), this means you are responsible for it.

It's great when an adolescent displays responsibility. Even children are given duties to help them learn responsibility and to show that everyone pitches in to keep the household running smoothly. Furthermore, being responsible leads to greater maturity and pride in one's abilities.

It has to begin with you handling small things that have fewer consequences, of course, but that doesn't mean they aren't important. Of course, no one will give you keys to the car anytime soon; it's too big a responsibility. You have to start small with things like doing your own studying, cleaning, and tidying up.

More responsibilities will be added as you grow older and keep showing you can deal with them. However, this also means you'll have more freedom! When you are in charge of your life, you have a lot of responsibility, but you are also free to make your own choices.

THE IMPORTANCE OF RESPONSIBILITY

In addition to attending to one's personal needs, taking personal responsibility also means accepting the consequences of your actions, whether good or negative. It's knowing and being okay with the results of your choices and actions. These behaviors include showing concern for yourself and others, feeling in charge, and remaining confident in your abilities. A responsible person cares about the well-being of those around them and takes action when necessary to provide for them.

Why is it important?

When you're growing up, you don't really understand how the world works. Every experience is new, even though you're discovering your bodies. Responsibility teaches you how to face the world and gives you an understanding of the life you're growing into. Learning responsibility helps you build leadership, communication, and social abilities and increases your ability to be receptive to new relationships, information, and perspectives.

Some of the benefits of personal responsibility include:

You will form a lasting connection with your family: When you're responsible, more duties and privileges will be extended to you. For example, your parents might ask you and your siblings to clean the house while they are away, leaving you in charge. Since you are in control, your siblings have to work with you, and depending on how you treat them, you are forming a deeper bond with them. When you complete the work, your parents will be happy with you and your siblings.

You become kinder: Remember that you are not flawless and will make mistakes; knowing and understanding that is vital to becoming kinder. It's not hard to see why compassion and responsibility go hand in hand. A kind and responsible person can put themselves in another person's shoes and respond appropriately. As a result, you will have the selflessness and care for others to help your loved ones when in need.

You understand that you can't control everything: Being responsible means you will sometimes fail and will be accountable. This failure shows that you can't control everything, and it's an excellent lesson to learn early. Life sometimes throws us curveballs, but through responsibility, you know not to try and do everything, just what is necessary. Trying to do everything and be everywhere at once is mentally and physically draining.

You can learn how to multitask effectively: Responsible people also make plans, prioritize tasks, and set objectives so they can learn to multitask well. Those who have learned how to take charge of their own lives can keep their cool under pressure and do more, regardless of the circumstances.

You'll learn to stay positive: Some people constantly complain about almost everything, and others do what they need to do without saying anything. No one enjoys interacting with a negative person who always finds something to complain about. Personal responsibility develops your ability to endure challenging conditions while being positive.

You won't blame others: No matter how well-prepared you are, things will sometimes go wrong. Instead of putting blame on someone else, you will always look for ways to improve circumstances and tackle problems as they arise. You have already learned to remain accountable so you can stay truthful whatever happens.

You grow into a dependable leader: Leaders are typically careful in taking action and maintaining a commitment. In addition, reliable people help people work together well. When you're responsible, others will rely on your judgment in many situations. In contrast to entitlement, responsibility is a privilege.

MAKING GOOD CHOICES

You will constantly be making decisions that you should stand by as you become more responsible. Some of these decisions will be simple and don't require much thought, while others are much more difficult. The ability to make good decisions is vital to all areas of your life, including your mood and even health. Here are some tips to help you out:

Refrain from reacting quickly: When you are faced with any situation and need to make a decision, don't jump into it. Never let the situation force you to make wrong on-the-spot decisions.

Don't let stress take over your life: Before facing any situation, learn to stay calm. Making tough decisions can be overwhelming and cause stress and anxiety. You will only make good decisions if you're relaxed, so try to handle your stress to avoid messing up your thinking.

Take a break: To take your time with decision-making and avoid stress and anxiety, you should relax. One way to achieve this is to set your problem aside for a while before deciding. This will help you feel sure about the choice you make. You could walk, sleep, or even listen to music quietly.

Weigh the positives and negatives: Look at the issue at hand after your break. View it as a whole, both the good and bad sides. You can even write them down. Look at all the pros and cons, and make sure you take them into account before you make a choice.

Prioritize: You should know what you want and what is most important. When you focus on what really matters to you, you'll find it easier to make a clear choice.

Consider the result of different options: In breaking down the problem, look at all the possible solutions you're thinking about. Deciding on something can lead to many different results, and often, not all of them may be clear or direct. Make sure to write down the possible consequences of each choice.

Share your thoughts: Discuss the problem with your parents, siblings, or friends. When someone else looks at the problem, they could have a better view and understanding than you.

Write things down: It's easy to say that you will remember everything, but that is often untrue. Write down your thoughts to help keep track of them.

Compare ideas: You have come up with some solutions. Compare those with the ideas from other people.

Find common ground: After comparing, try to find common ground. There will be a unifying solution for you. And if you can't find common ground, trust your instincts.

Prepare for anything: Try to prepare for anything. Whether you believe you have made the right decision or not, you'll have to deal with the results.

HONESTY IS THE
BEST POLICY

Being honest is more than just not lying or cheating; it's about speaking and acting truthfully in all situations. It means treating others with respect and being open and aware of your actions.

Importance of Being Honest

Being truthful helps us remain genuine in our relationships with others and ourselves. Some advantages of honesty include values such as kindness, self-control, moral integrity, truthfulness, and compassion. When you develop these qualities, you build genuine connections with others and live without confrontations. So, in the long run, you realize you are surrounded by people you can trust.

Honesty separates you from trouble: There are troubles people would have safely avoided if they had told the truth. Honesty is the best policy in any circumstance, no matter how challenging. Lying to people may seem convenient or easy, but when the truth comes to light, you'll lose the trust — and respect — of others.

Honesty leads to peace: Because of your truthfulness, you will enjoy peace around and in your mind. We have discussed that it separates you from trouble, so you don't have to be worried about anything. You remain peaceful when you have always been truthful and have never misled anyone. There is no shame and worry to feel, hence the rewarding peace.

You can simplify your life: When you lie, you will find that you have to keep coming up with more lies to cover the previous ones. This takes a lot of work and grows more complex, and now you have to keep up with it, and you may find yourself leading a double existence.

Honesty makes you believable: Being truthful in all situations lends credibility to what you say. When you compliment or try to boost others' spirits, they'll know you genuinely mean it.

You stop being fake: When people know you are always truthful, they draw closer to you. When they draw closer, they can learn more about the true you. Being honest about everything will make you stand out—in a good way.

Being truthful can boost one's self-esteem. Consider those who tend to say what's on their minds. It's as if they don't censor their thoughts at all. It's hard to claim that someone who is always truthful lacks self-assurance. You should be confident to express yourself openly without worrying about other people's reactions.

People tend to respect you: Being honest about our identities, strengths, and weaknesses is crucial. This demonstrates that we act with honesty. It stands to reason that if you discovered someone you admired had exaggerated their good characteristics, you would lose respect for them. Respect must be cultivated by protecting against dishonesty at all costs.

People tend to trust you: Since people respect you, their interactions with you are essentially based on trust. When you are genuine, those around you feel they can be themselves and trust you entirely. Keeping faith in those close to us is essential. Once trust has been damaged, it may not be easy (or even possible) to repair.

People will like you: When people can trust you, they become honest with you and eventually like you. This process will make it almost impossible for such a relationship to break, and as a young boy, these are relationships you should desire to form. Sometimes, people tell lies to win the favor of others around them. This never works because when people like us because of our lies, they don't really know who we are. Also, if someone decides they don't like you because of your falsehoods, you'll never know if they would have appreciated you anyway if you'd just been honest. Genuine connections can only be made when everyone involved is comfortable enough to be themselves around one another.

Honesty increases your chance of success: It's worth considering whether or not you can get what you want by being honest. Just be more direct about what you want, and don't hesitate to ask for it.

CHAPTER ELEVEN: PEER PRESSURE AND BULLYING

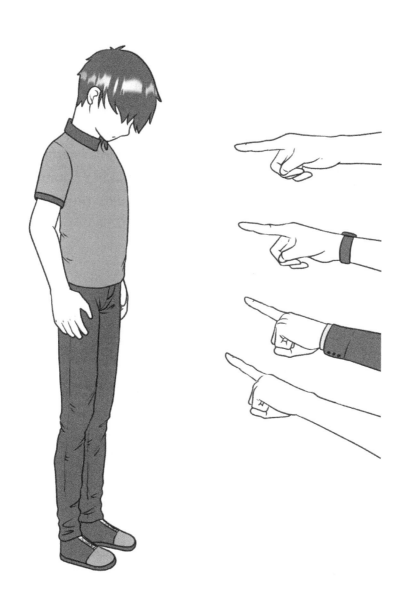

Teenagers are often sociable beings who take pleasure in being in the company of other people, just like everyone else. You will have a strong urge to interact with other people when you are a teenager, and you may choose to act on that desire. On the other hand, this may put you in a spot that needs you to work to overcome challenges. To develop and progress, you need to establish guidelines for how you should interact with other people.

We've already discussed how being honest makes more people want to interact with you and increases the quality of every relationship you have. The influence that the people in your life have on your choices is the primary focus of this chapter. You may think that no one will ever force you into making poor choices, but many people have made poor choices *because* they thought they were immune to the influence of others. It begins with pressure from peers and then escalates into bullying.

STANDING UP FOR YOURSELF

Peer Pressure

Did you know that "peers" are basically people who are around your age? Your classmates, the kids in your neighborhood, and your friends are all examples of your peers. You gain so much information just by hanging out with each other all the time. Have you ever felt like you were forced to do something just because your friends were doing it? That's called *peer pressure*. It happens when your friends influence you to take action. Your friends will have a big impact on the decisions you make, whether good or bad.

Good peer pressure: This is when someone encourages you to do something good, like being kind to others, working hard in school, helping at home, or staying away from alcohol and drugs. Your friends can encourage you to make good choices and do the right thing. When your friends encourage you to study in school or care for others in your community, that's positive peer pressure. It's essential to surround yourself with friends who positively influence you.

Bad peer pressure: This is when one of your peers tries to convince you to do something that's bad for you or that's harmful to others. This could be skipping class, lying, bullying, stealing, cheating, or drinking alcohol. Sometimes, you might feel pressured to do something you don't want to do because you want to fit in and be popular. However, just because others are doing something doesn't mean it's a good idea. This could happen if someone offers you something in exchange, challenges you, keeps asking, or threatens you. It's important to be able to recognize when someone is pressuring you to do something harmful.

Bullying

Bullying is a common issue between peers during adolescence. Bullying happens when someone repeatedly bothers, teases, or annoys another person or group.

Did you know bullies often lack empathy for their victims and don't feel bad about bullying them? When someone is bullied, they often feel awful about themselves. They might not feel very popular or successful in school. They will have a very difficult time adjusting to things.

It's important to remember that bullying can have serious consequences, and treating someone poorly is never okay. Bullying can take on many different forms. It might involve calling someone names, spreading nasty rumors about them, or even physically hurting them.

How Bad Peer Pressure Becomes Bullying

Let's use smoking as an example. It is a common issue that occurs to a lot of young people. When adolescents see their peers smoking, they might feel pressured to join because they feel that smoking will help them fit in. Peer pressure becomes bullying when an adolescent is pressured to smoke, and they say no, and the group keeps pressuring them to the point of making them feel bad for not smoking. That has become bullying.

The Importance of Standing Up for Yourself

Being able to protect yourself doesn't necessarily mean you have to fight people. It's more about standing up for yourself and not letting other people or situations make you feel bad about yourself. Standing up to bullying makes you a stronger person who can better deal with sadness, anxiety, fear, confusion, and more.

You should stand up for yourself because you are a source of joy to someone; imagine how those who care about you will feel when they learn that you have been mistreated by others and they couldn't do anything about it. Remember, you have or will have siblings, friends, and possibly children of your own who will look up to you for protection, so you want to develop yourself enough to fulfill that role for them.

HANDLING
BULLIES

You have to be able to stand up for yourself if you want to deal with bullies or mean people.

Be confident: The last lesson talks about how crucial it is to stand up for yourself. However, you can only stand up for yourself if you have enough confidence. Part of the reason people become bullies is that they don't have much faith in themselves, so they try to hurt people they think are weaker than them. They do this to make themselves feel strong, even though they aren't. If you don't want to be or remain a victim, you have to stand up to them and show that you are not weaker and that they are not better than you — but you can only do all these things if you understand that you are a good person who deserves happiness.

Know that you are strong: You can still be scared even if you're sure of yourself; however, these bullies are people just like you. They are not unique in any way. Some may be taller or bigger than you, but that doesn't make them better. Understand that they are weak because they could be good to people but choose to be mean because they think it's easier. So, use your fear as motivation to stand up to bullies.

Tell a grown-up: People are angry about bullying, especially now that many adults have talked about the bad things bullies did to them on social media and how it hurt them. So, when someone in charge hears about bullying, they don't take it lightly. Talk to someone, like your parents, a teacher, or the school counselor. Don't let fear stop you from telling someone who can help you or get you help. If someone is hurting you physically and you are in danger, you should talk to an adult immediately. If that adult doesn't do anything, go tell someone else. Things they should know are:

- Who started the bullying?
- Where and when did it happen?
- What is being done about it?
- For how long has the bullying been going on?
- How it has made you feel.

Don't stop telling people about it. Adults who were bullied as kids always regret not talking about it when it happened.

Learn not to react: Walk away when the bully approaches you. You're not scared; you just don't care. This bully or bullies aren't important, and you shouldn't waste your time on them. By leaving the room, you can think about something else.

Be nice to other people: When someone is trying hard to be negative, remember all the good things you are capable of doing and can say. You may be surprised later when someone you helped or were nice to long ago remembers and helps you when you need it.

Make friends: This helps you get along with others, but it also makes it hard for bullies to pick on or get close to you. If you're always with other people, they'll be right there to stand up for you if you are bullied or mistreated. Use the buddy system to stop bullying; bullies feel they have the right to pick on one person, but they rarely pick on a group. Spend time with your friends but be sure to choose friends who are good and kind.

KINDNESS AND RESPECT

Treating others with respect and kindness means finding the good in them and helping them see their own value. It's being able to see the possibility of great things in everyone, believing in that goodness, and using it to relate to people even when they don't or can't see what they could be.

Kindness: Kindness is the decision to act in a way that benefits another person out of genuine feelings of warmth. Kindness frequently means putting the needs of others over our own.

Respect: Respect is one of the most crucial moral principles for a fulfilling life. Having respect for others is treating them with kindness and regard no matter what their background is.

- Learning to treat others well is the first step to building good relationships.
- You change for the better and remain positive.
- When you do the work to be kind to others, you can make a difference, especially for people who are weak or suffering.
- You often find out about traits and skills you didn't know you had.
- Kindness also makes you feel less stressed, boosts your self-worth, and makes you happier.
- You can see life from different wonderful points of view when you make new friends and learn about their lives.

- People will say nice things about you publicly because you have good traits.

- You help people develop the gifts they have.

- It lessens unfairness and injustice.

- It makes people understand that they belong and feel less alone.

- This lifestyle makes the world a better place, and one act of kindness often leads to more.

- When you are available to assist others, you also help yourself.

- It feels good to treat other people well!

CHAPTER TWELVE: GOALS AND AMBITIONS

Everyone has goals in life, whether they involve a career, family, or a personal trait, they want to develop. When you have a goal, it's easy to concentrate on the steps you need to take to achieve each objective. Goals help you make plans for the future, efficiently using the resources available to you, such as time and money. They help you see which things you can do yourself and where you'll need to work with others. Goals and ambitions give you something to reach for, a cause to appreciate, and a reason to stay motivated.

WORKING TOWARD GOALS

As you grow up, you'll learn the importance of having ambitions and goals. It's hard to get anywhere in life when you don't know where you want to go. Setting targets for yourself is as essential as knowing how to reach them. Pursuing the right goal can help you succeed and simplify any other challenges.

Improved focus: When you know what you want and set your plans to achieve it, it can help you do better work because you can focus your effort on reaching your goal. This way, you're not just trying everything to find what falls in place and what doesn't.

Reduced procrastination: Because you are less distracted, you'll find it easier to get started and keep going, even when things get tough. Having a goal keeps you motivated.

Better time management: When you're not confused about what to do next, you don't have to waste time trying to figure it out. Because this is your ambition and not something you're being forced to do, you'll be motivated to see it through. It'll be easy to make a schedule to manage your time in the best way possible. One thing you can do in order to manage your time is to break your goals down into steps.

Increased contribution: You read about responsibility earlier in this book, part of which involves helping your family, community, and friends. Having goals encourages you to be responsible even when nobody is around; this will translate to things that other people want you to do.

Better accountability: Now you are responsible for your goals, and as a result, you learn to be accountable. If you decide to be serious about your goals and ambitions, you'll keep yourself on track, even when you don't have to report your progress to anyone. If they're important to you, you owe it to yourself and nobody else to be accountable.

A continuous growth mindset: You should strive to develop what is known as a growth mindset, which means you'll always look back at what you did well and try to find ways to improve where you need it.

Progressive living: Learning to set and reach goals can help you find ways to balance your education, health, and social life.

Major key points to hold on to:

- Believe in yourself more as you go along.
- Figure out how you work best and do that.
- Find ways to stay motivated.
- Keep going even when things are tough.
- Don't be afraid to ask for help.

DISCOVERING YOUR PASSIONS

Start with your hobbies: What do you have fun doing? Growing up, you probably found many things that you enjoyed doing. Discovering something you are passionate about is easier because you are young and mostly rely on instincts, so you know whatever you are doing, you are doing because you love it. Something you enjoy doing is your hobby, and your hobby can easily be seen as your passion; you just need to find a way to work that into a career.

Find your talents: What things can you do effortlessly, and will you do well? These will be things that align with your natural abilities, abilities you are born with; for example, singing really well is a natural ability. Many successful musicians have reportedly talked about how they started singing very early with no training whatsoever. You always need to develop a natural ability, but it's a lot easier if you enjoy doing it.

The things you learn about: We're not just talking about school! There are things you love to hear about or learn more about, some of which you will read about or watch videos about online. Spend time exploring these options. This could be your passion, and more research may point you in the right direction. It makes sense that you will encounter many things that pique your interest, so keep an open mind about them all.

Try different perspectives: Perhaps you are unsure of your passion, but you can try a little brainstorming with a pen and paper, ready to jot down any ideas that pop up. Putting your thoughts on paper is helpful because it helps your brain process things better, and you can always refer back to them. Moving around also helps stimulate new ideas. If studying in one area doesn't seem to be working for you, try moving to a different one. Watch videos, go online, read books, do things you love to do, and when ideas come, jot them down.

Look at your circle: The people you hang out with often show where your interest lies. If you note what your friends are interested in and you enjoy them also, this could be pointing to something you are passionate about. The truth is that minds that are alike attract, and friends are people of like minds who often have things in common.

Talk to adults: There are people around you who are more experienced than you. You can have real discussions with them when you have the opportunity, whether you have found your passion or not. If you have found your passion, share this with people who may know more about it. If you haven't discovered what you want to do, have simple discussions with people who spark your interest. Whether it's about hobbies, careers, or something entirely different, listen and ask questions. Keep your options open.

Continuous practice: When things come naturally to you, it can be easy to take them for granted. If you start to feel you have begun to take them for granted, it's time to change your process and mindset; start by seeing the need to continue your hobbies or sharpen your skills. If you still need to get an idea of what you want to do, practice the process again and again until you know what you want.

Invest in new things: Don't be opposed to new hobbies. Start new things and be positive when your friends think up new things to do—as long as they are the proper things to do. If there are things you don't like, you have learned about peer pressure; it's not hard to say no.

Never give up: Keep trying until you find what you want because if you quit, you might miss out on being truly happy doing what you love. Don't give up, whether it takes a long time or not, because you will eventually get it. Even if you find something you like but after a while, you discover you don't want to do it for a long time, you can try again and find something else. Also, trying many things and keeping notes about those experiences is an excellent way to reflect on your journey and determine if you need to make any changes.

KEEPING A POSITIVE ATTITUDE

It's important to stay positive at every point, even when not everything is going so well. Your thoughts can affect your overall mental state and, therefore, affect what you do. Think positive thoughts, and you'll notice remarkable changes happening around you. When you think positively, you'll see the world differently. You can control your feelings and learn from every challenging situation you face.

Positivity comes in various forms, so here are some tips to remain positive:

Be brave: Moving forward despite being afraid is important to achieving your dreams. Of course, times will come when you might be frightened to try, and you may even fail, but mistakes sometimes lead to success. Mistakes and failures are valuable because they teach us things we might not learn otherwise, so no matter how many mistakes you make, keep trying until success comes your way.

Be confident: You are the one in charge of your life. It's you who makes things happen. If you believe in who you are and, in your dreams, as this book has discussed, you should be strong. You're young, and anything can happen, so be confident.

Be diligent: Hard work is one of the ingredients in the recipe for success. Believing in your goals and dreams pushes you to work hard to realize them. The diligence with which you pursue your dreams will help you achieve them. Just thinking about your dreams won't bring you any closer to them. Refrain from avoiding your problems. Deal with them. Putting in the energy and time will make your dreams come true.

Take risks: Being a risk-taker means you risk losing something important to you for a greater reward. You shouldn't just take any risk, though; taking calculated risks, meaning you consider your decision carefully, is a better way to become a successful person. Risk-taking involves opening your mind to exploring new and unfamiliar circumstances. Even though you feel uncertain, you'll gain something important, maybe a new skill. Examples of risk-taking include trying out for the school play, entering a singing competition, joining a band, and signing up for educational competitions. It could even be as simple as raising your hand to answer a question in class.

Be positive: One great advantage of taking risks is that it prepares you to be accepting of any result. Whether the outcome could be good or bad, you are positive about how you will react.

Keep at it: Keep going; that's the simplest way of achieving anything. Whether you have a picture of success or not, keep doing it. There will always be challenges to overcome, but this is the story most people tell! It's not just about achieving your goals; it's about the journey you take to get there. Giving up means there is no hope of achieving anything at all.

CHAPTER THIRTEEN: CONCLUSION

Congratulations on getting to this point! You've learned a lot in this book, starting with the fact that your body changing is simply puberty. The changes you will experience (or are already experiencing) are a normal part of growing up. Some boys' physical changes will be faster or slower than others; the physical changes will also differ. Every person will have a unique experience with puberty. Some major experiences include voice changes, the development of acne or pimples, and growing pains.

Puberty is the perfect time to learn about the male reproductive system. Now you understand everything that is going on down there. We have explored the concept of sex as something between two humans caring for one another to bring babies into the world.

So, now you know that your feelings are essential and are often intense and all over the place during puberty. You know that this is because of hormones, such as testosterone, being released in higher quantities. You know that it's okay to express these emotions but that you also have to control your reactions to them. For example, the book discussed dealing with stress and anxiety, two powerful emotions you'll feel during puberty.

We have mentioned hormones, their importance during puberty, and the need to develop a personal hygiene regimen to deal with the consequences of development. Part of that regimen discussed in this book included washing your hands, brushing your teeth, and bathing regularly.

Aside from hygiene, you should not be surprised that you eat more during puberty, though you *have* learned that nutrition is very important. You also learned that you need to cut out junk food, which can lead to health challenges if you aren't careful. You have also seen the benefit of exercising, resting, and sleeping to avoid health problems and grow properly. These are critically necessary for a growing body; they keep you physically well and improve your mental health. We have expanded on the need to speak to adults at every point when you are stuck; they've gone through puberty, and they will understand your issues, especially when it comes to mental health.

Another contribution to excellent mental health is presenting yourself well by regularizing grooming. Washing your face, clipping your nails, cleaning your teeth, brushing your hair, and the other practices we discussed add a feeling of confidence and build your self-esteem. You are responsible for your own personal hygiene, grooming, exercise, and nutrition, among other things, which is why we also discussed the issue of personal responsibility. Knowing how it is sometimes difficult to make good choices, we provided details of how to make the right decision, remain accountable, and maintain honesty.

The chapter on peer pressure and bullying touched on not allowing others to force you into making bad decisions. By explaining peer pressure and bullying, we helped you understand why you should stand up for yourself against any form of pressure, whether from friends or bullies. In order to not end up like bullies, you have learned why it's important to treat others with respect and kindness.

The last chapter discussed why setting goals and working towards them is crucial; this can't be emphasized enough, especially as an adolescent. As you develop physically and mentally, you should also push yourself to be better by finding something you're passionate about and having a positive attitude that can help you achieve your dreams. Finally, one of the most important and easiest goals you can have is to be kind to yourself and others.

REACH OUT FOR HELP!

It's very important to have an adult, someone older who has passed through the stage of puberty just as you have, that you can talk to. You need these people around to talk to them about things like puberty, your emotions, mental health, and other general issues. These adults might be parents, grandparents, other family members, babysitters, teachers, school counselors, or coaches. Your friends' parents can help you with advice on tough questions and maybe even share their beliefs or religion.

No matter who the adult is, they should be there to help and support young people, especially those with extra difficulties with their bodies, feelings, or friends. In all fairness, it can be challenging for you to talk to some adults because you feel uncomfortable or worried that they will lecture you. However, you shouldn't let this stop you from reaching out to trusted adults who are ready and willing to listen to what you have to say.

Start with older siblings if you have any; if not, let your parents be your first go-to. If you feel like you aren't getting through to your parents, speak to a trusted teacher at school or a counselor. If all else fails, or it's a serious issue concerning your health, reach out to your doctor. Never at any point should you give up; when any of these people don't respond as they are supposed to, keep reaching out until you find a person willing to hear you out.

BE CONFIDENT OF
WHO YOU ARE!

You are great, important, and good enough—and yes, we wrote this guidebook to help you come to that understanding. Puberty comes with many emotions that tend to make adolescents like you feel less of themselves if they are not careful and are not taught to love themselves for who they are.

You are unique; your body is not the same as any other person's, so when you really think about it, you are truly special. It, therefore, makes sense that you embrace your uniqueness! Be confident, believe in who you are, and remain proud of yourself and who you will become because you are choosing to be that person. Don't allow anyone to reduce your self-esteem, primarily through the internet; social media has been used to cause many problems for adolescents, so don't become a victim. You can become who you dreamed of being and spread your positivity to the world!

Made in the USA
Coppell, TX
15 December 2024

42299998R00075